All these things happen
in one second and last for ever.

Virginia Woolf
The Waves

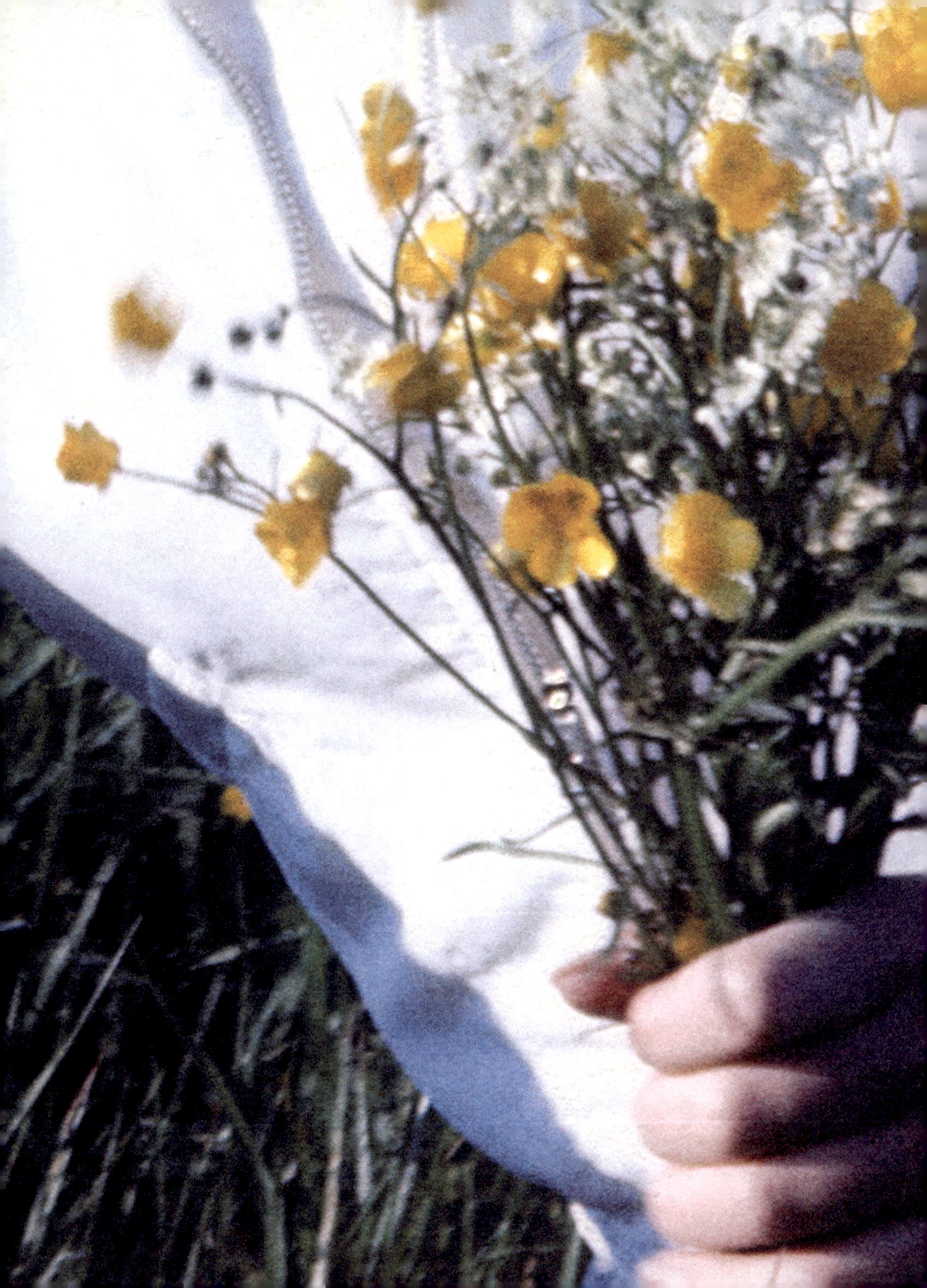

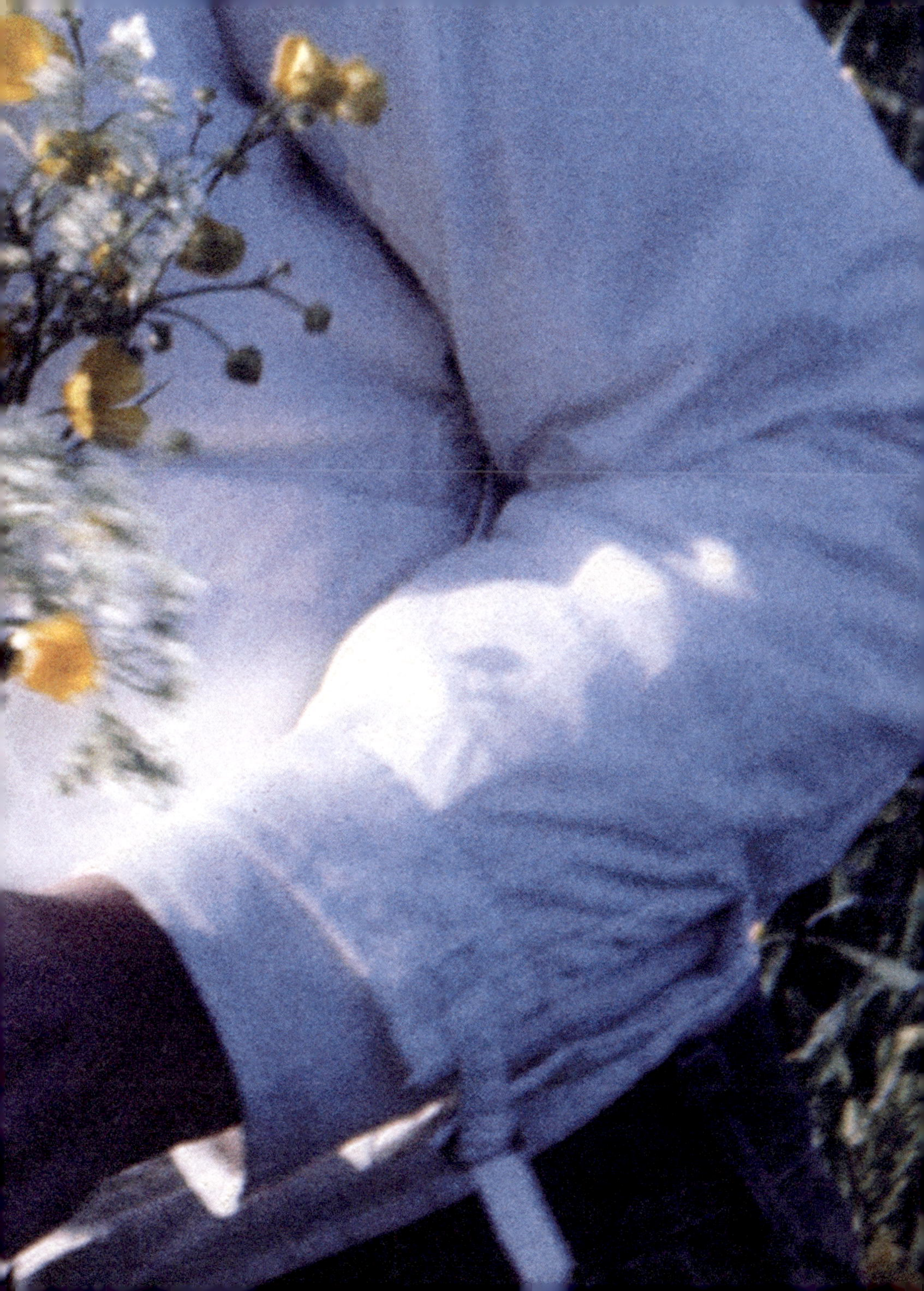

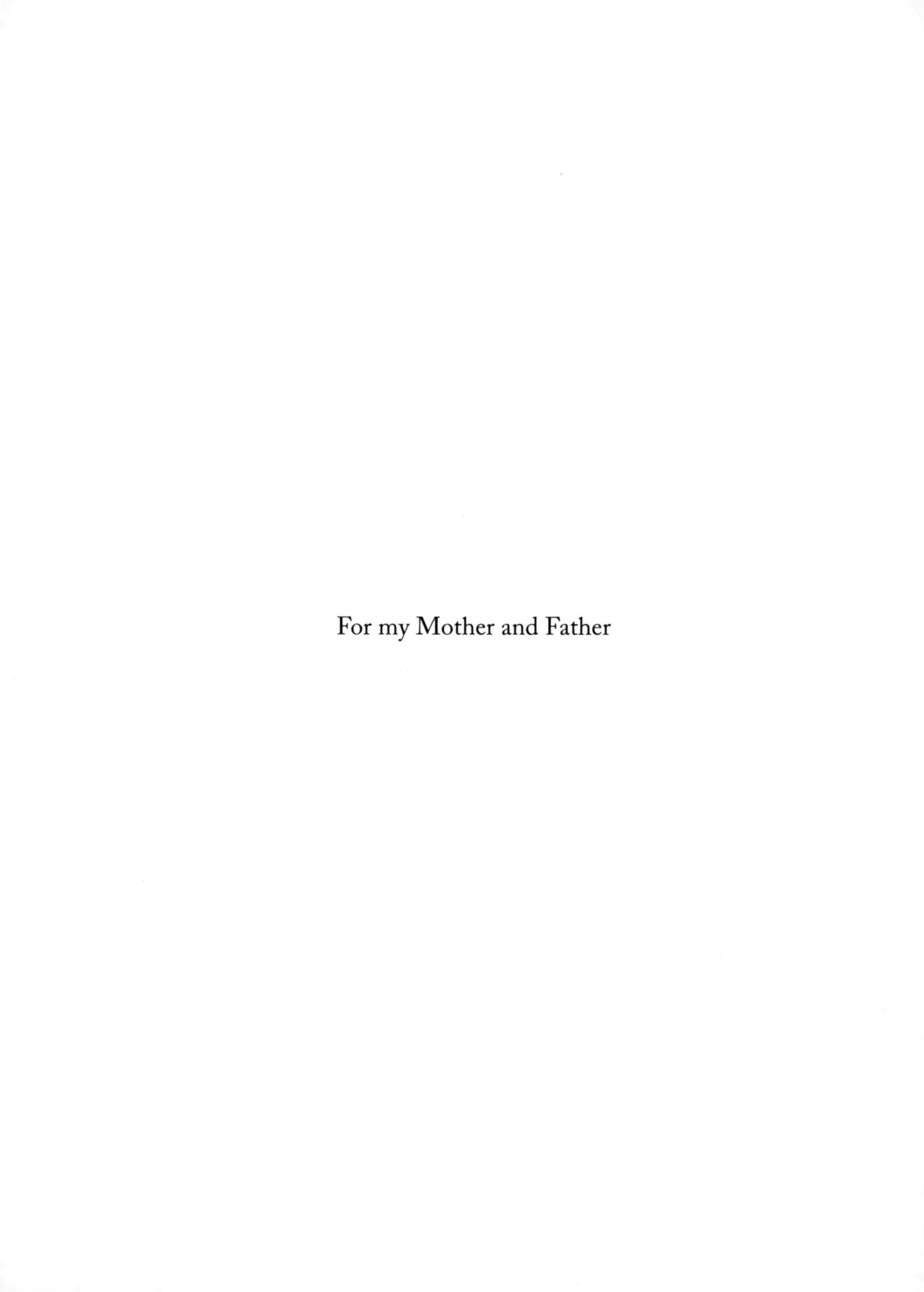

For my Mother and Father

THE MOTHERS I MIGHT HAVE HAD

Caroline Furneaux

DEWI LEWIS PUBLISHING

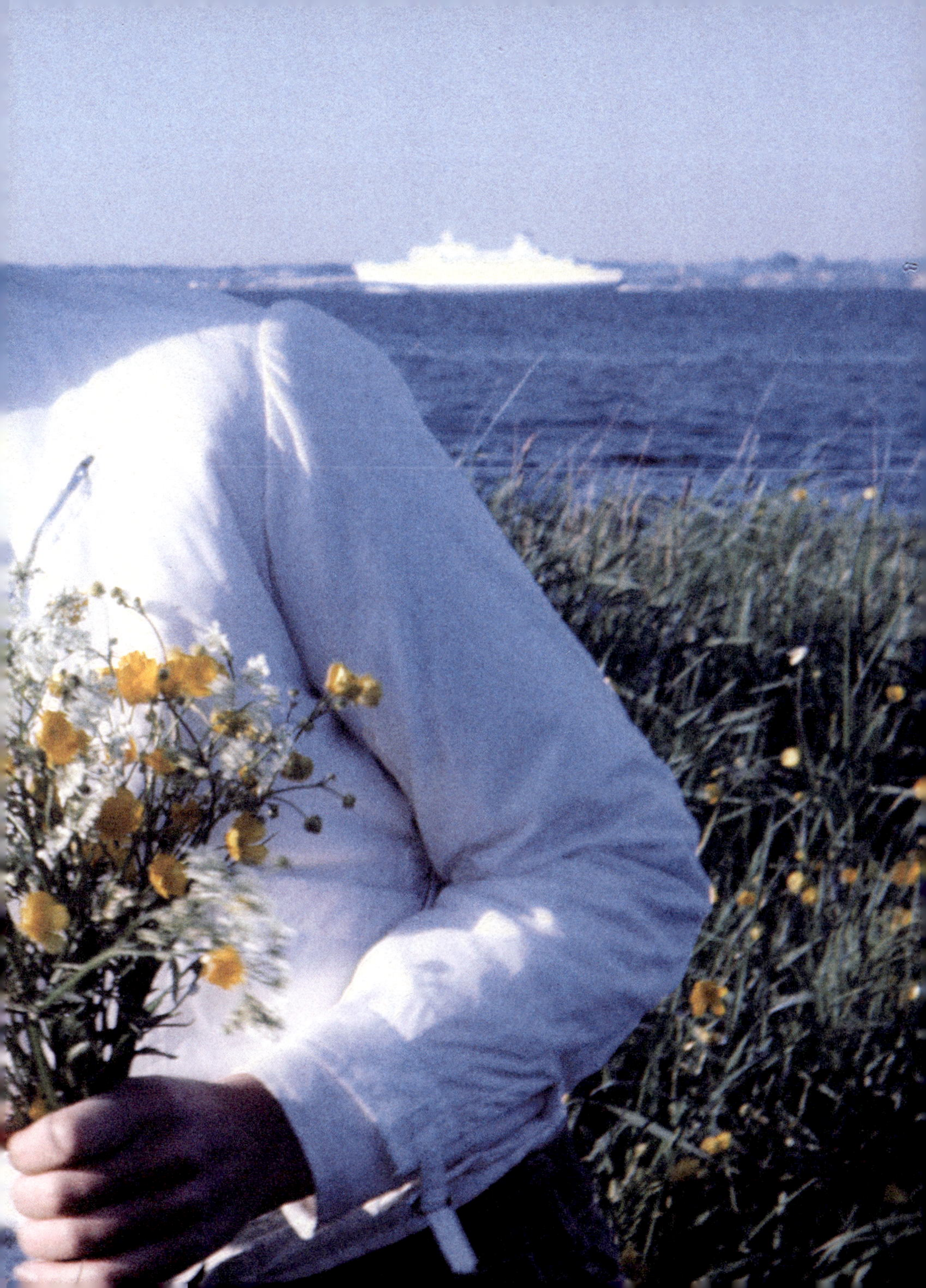

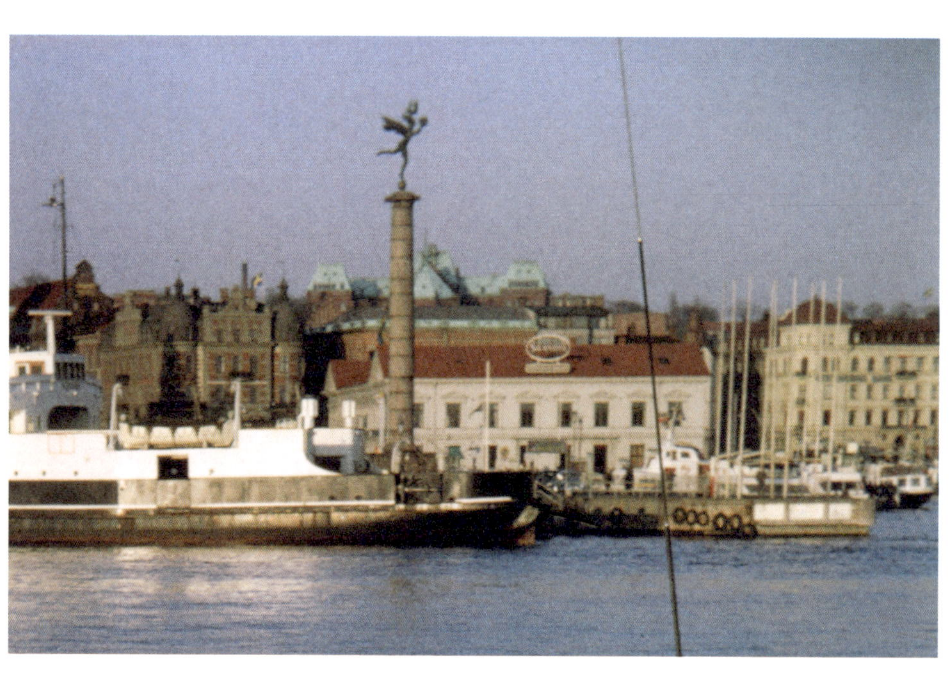

Helsingborg.

I recognise the green
bronze statue.

A female winged goddess.

She is carefully balancing
a ship in each hand,
as she soars into the sky.

BIBI

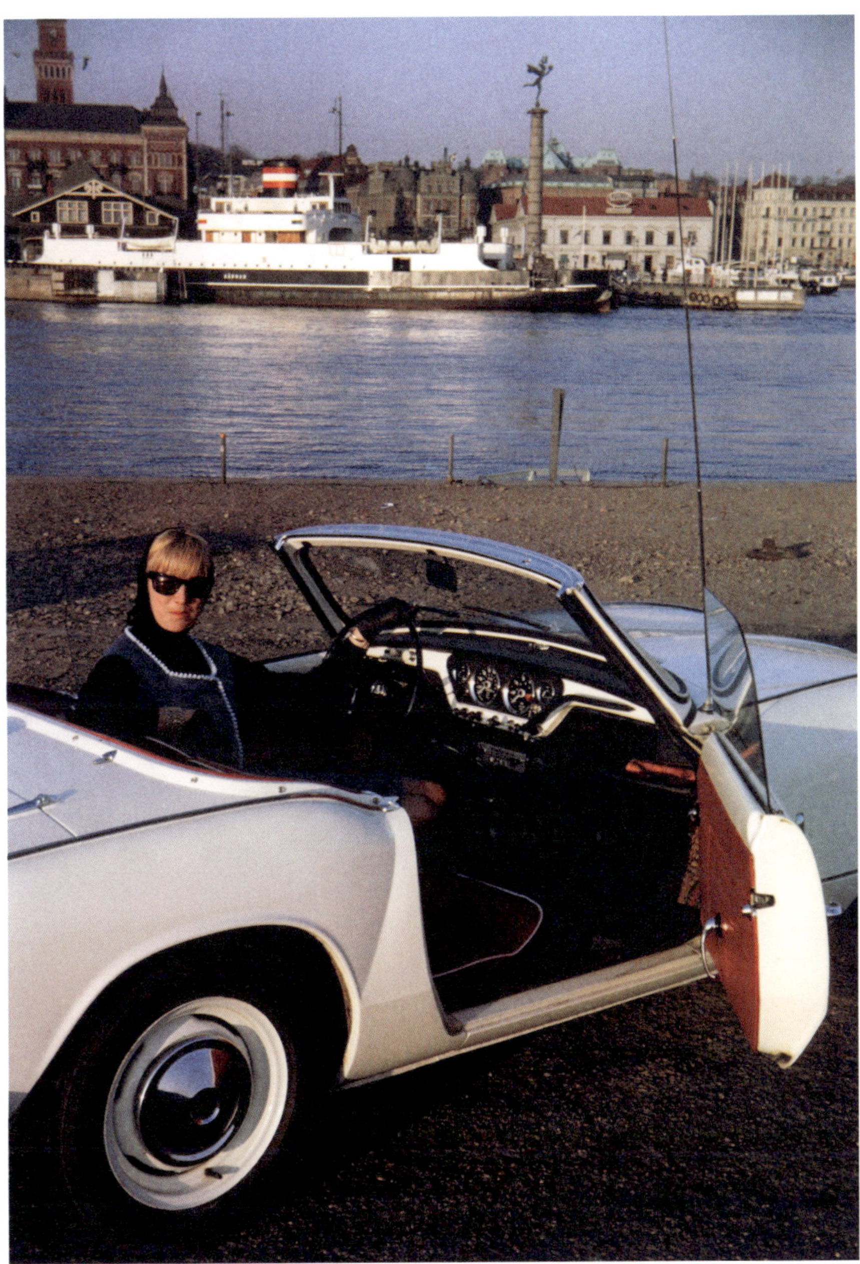

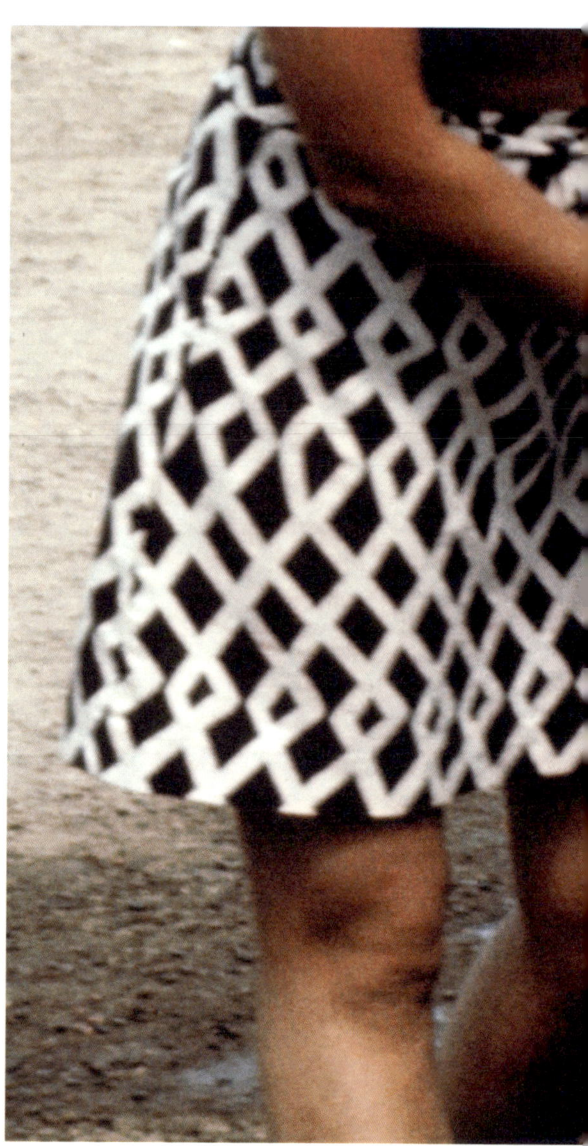

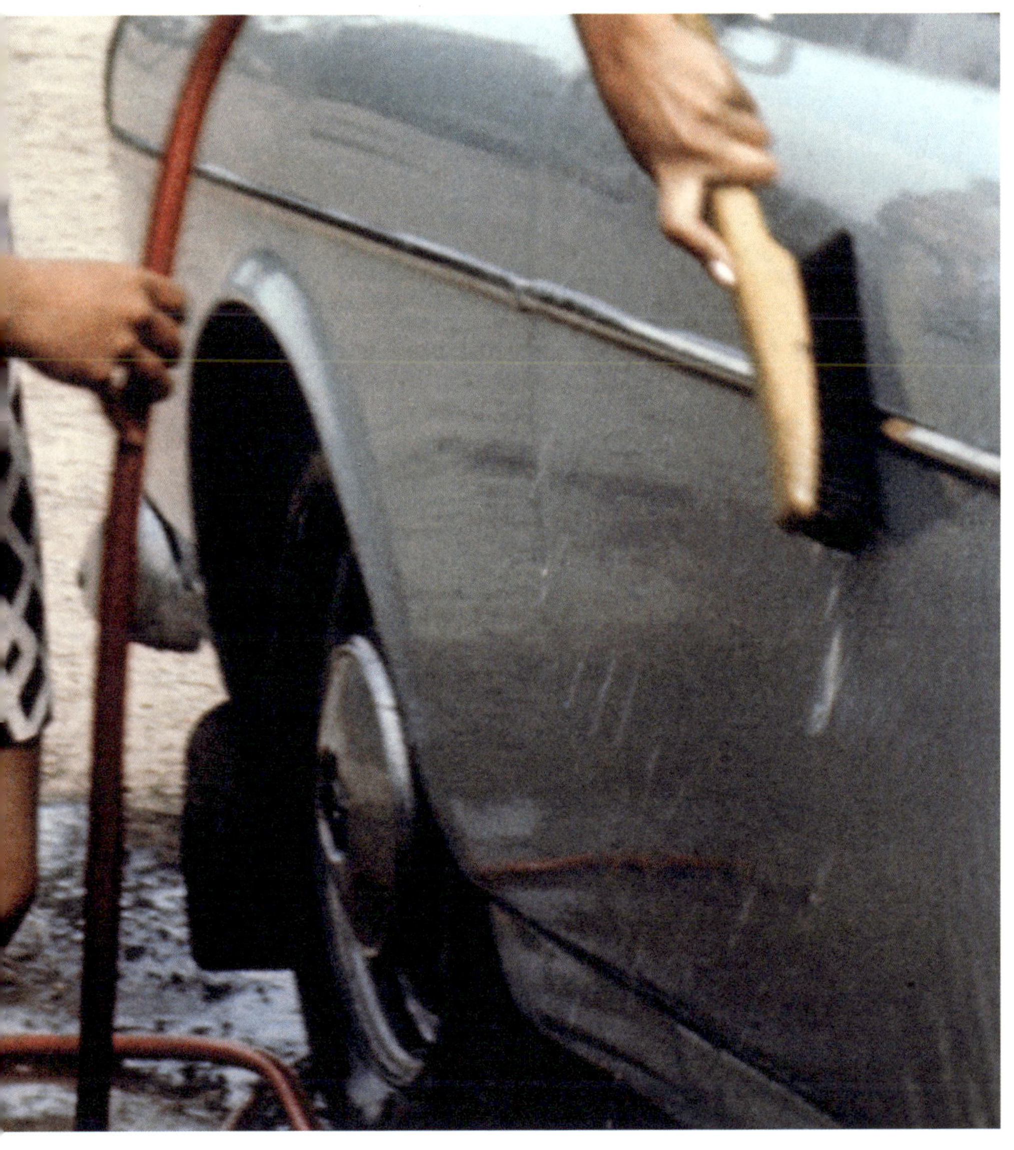

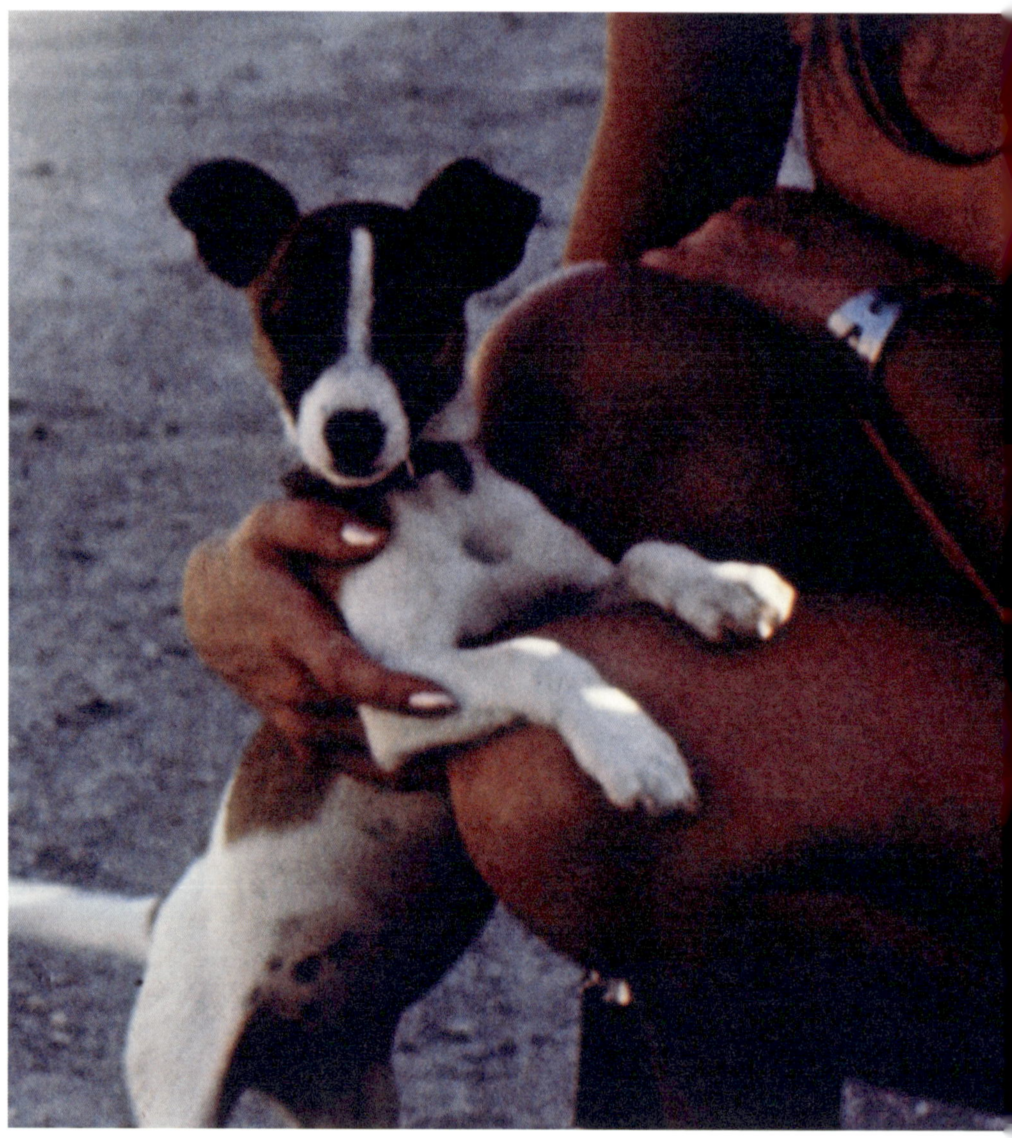

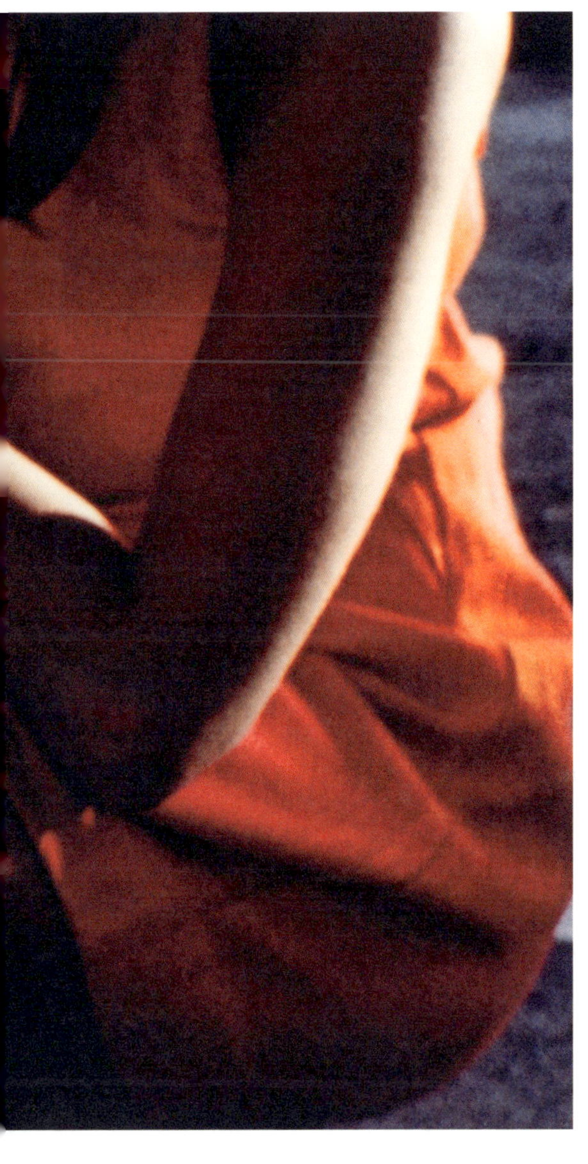

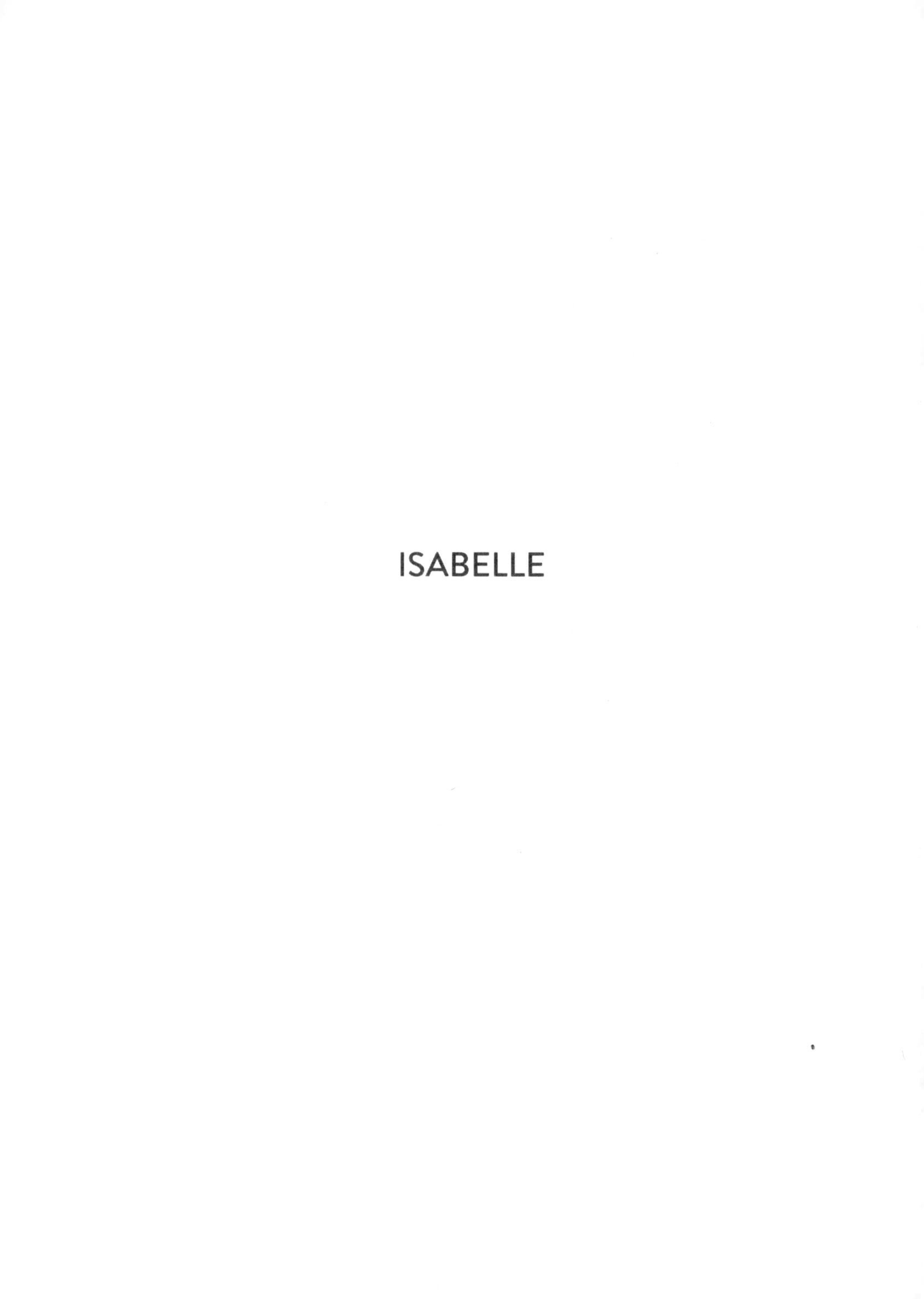

ISABELLE

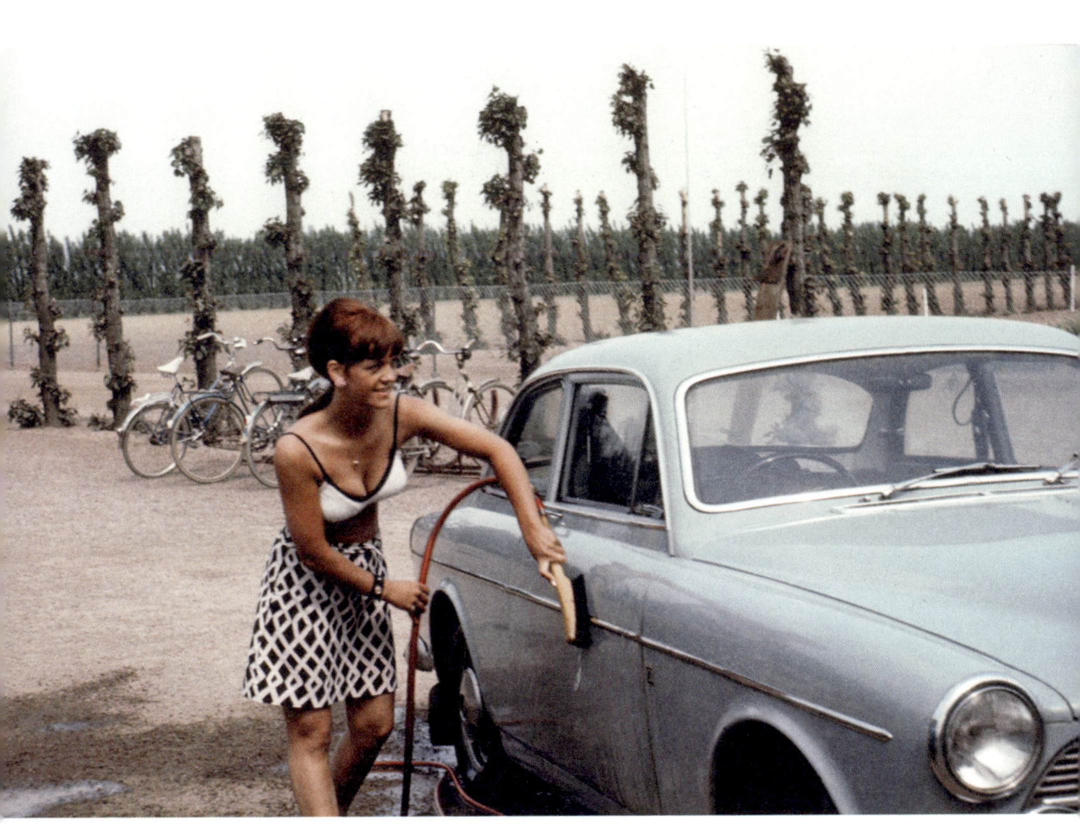

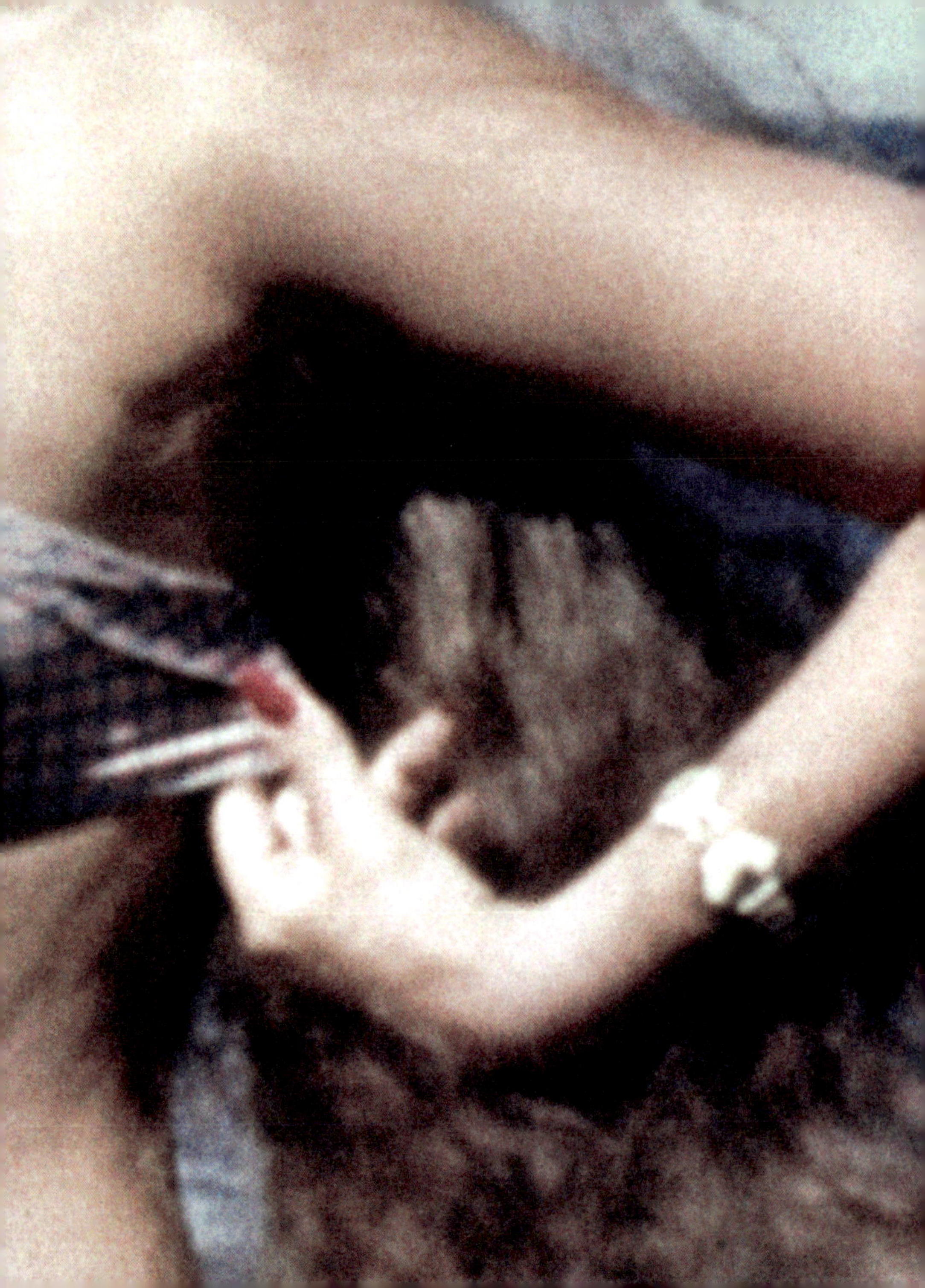

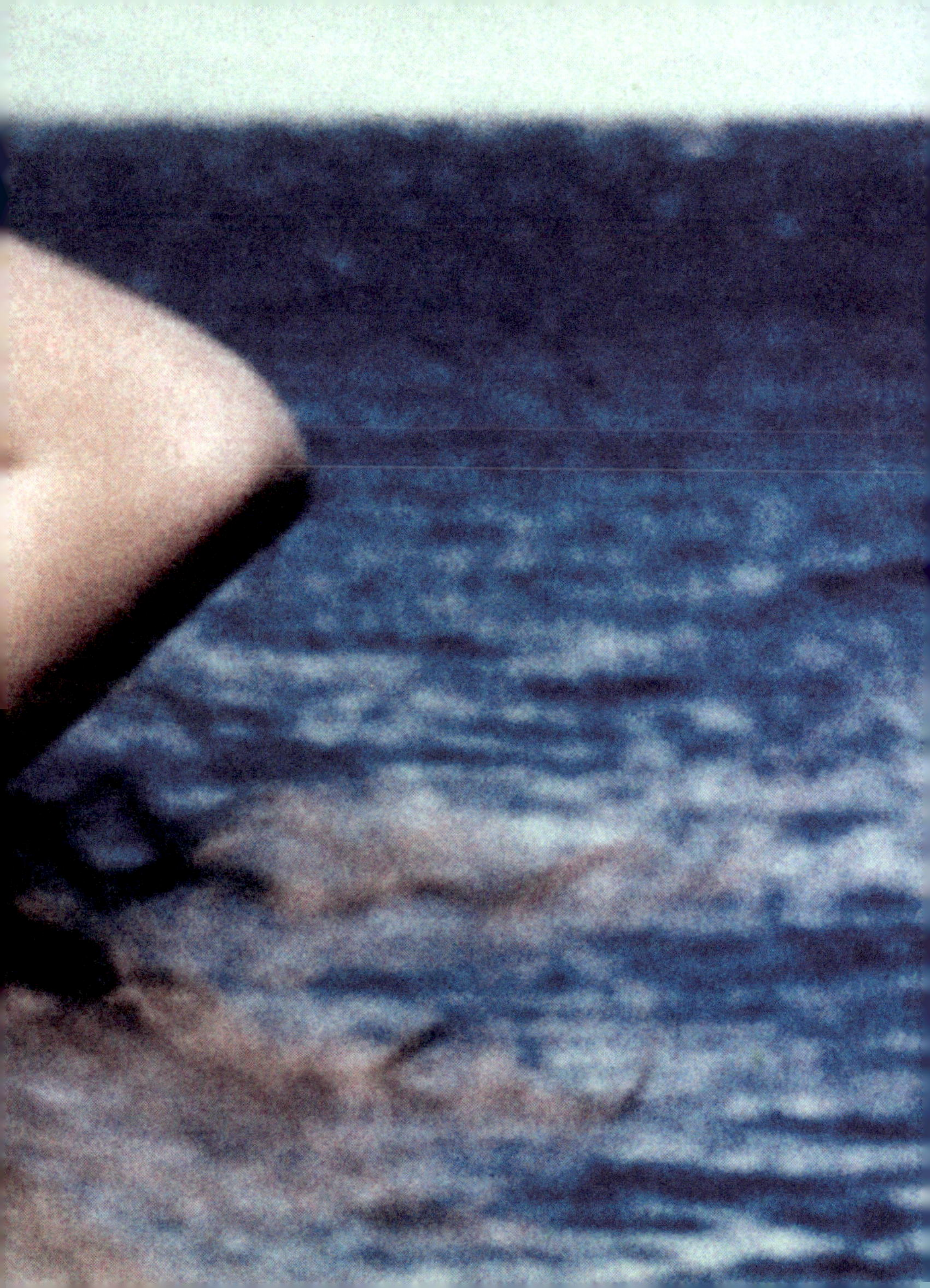

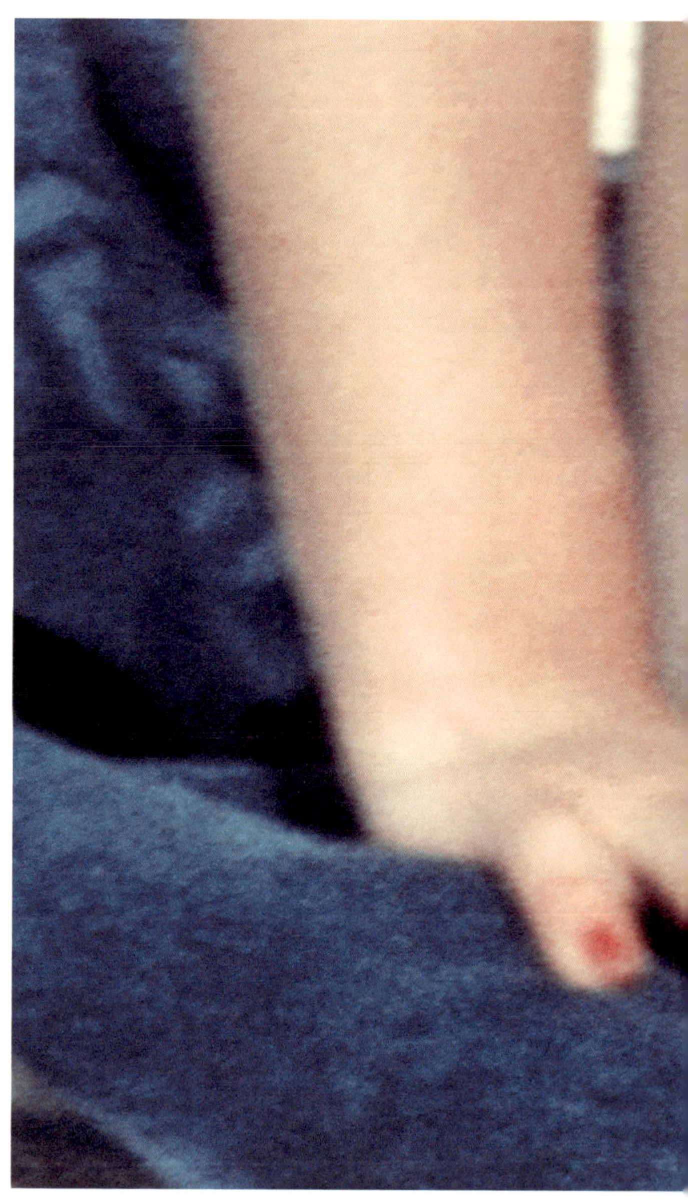

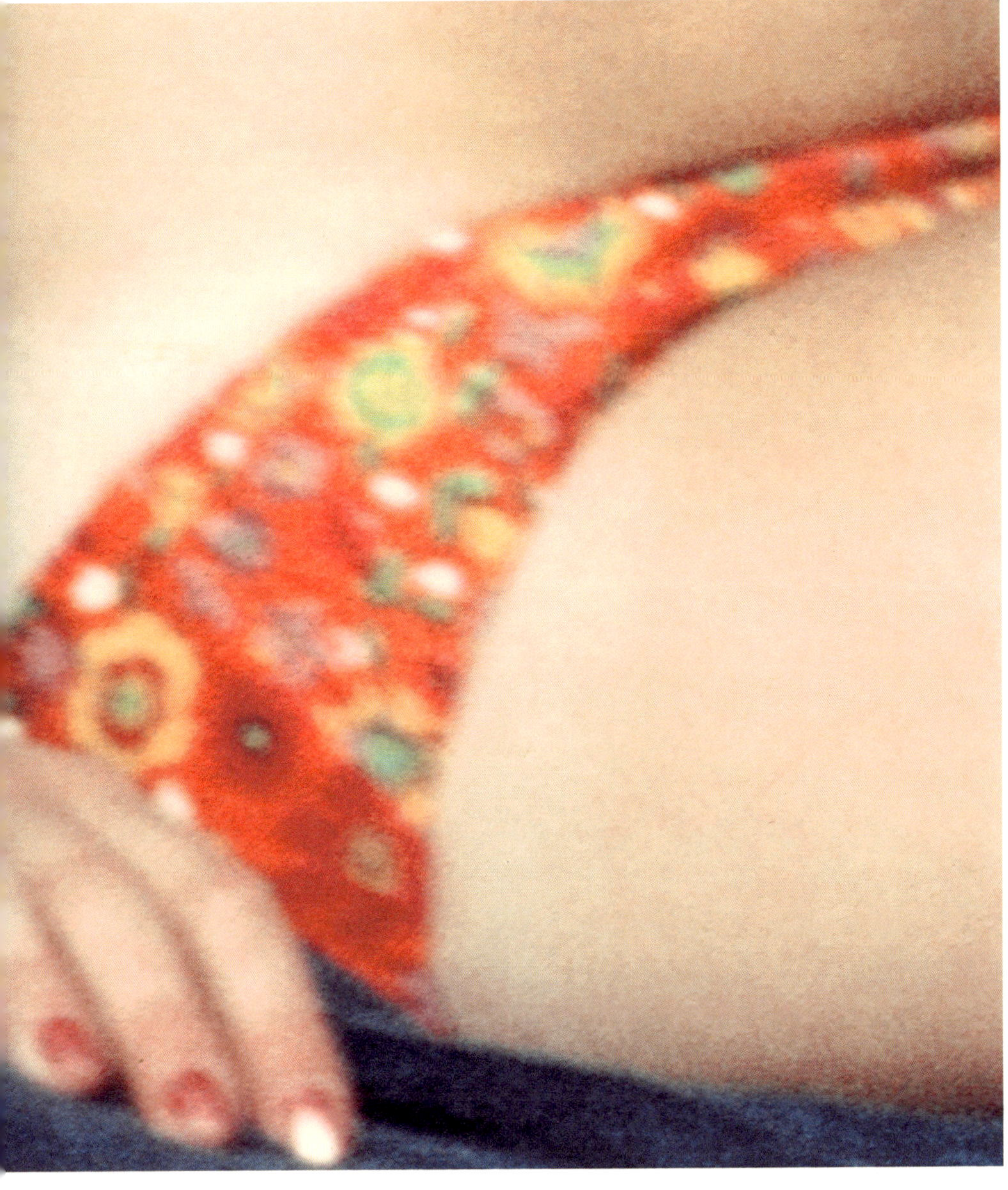

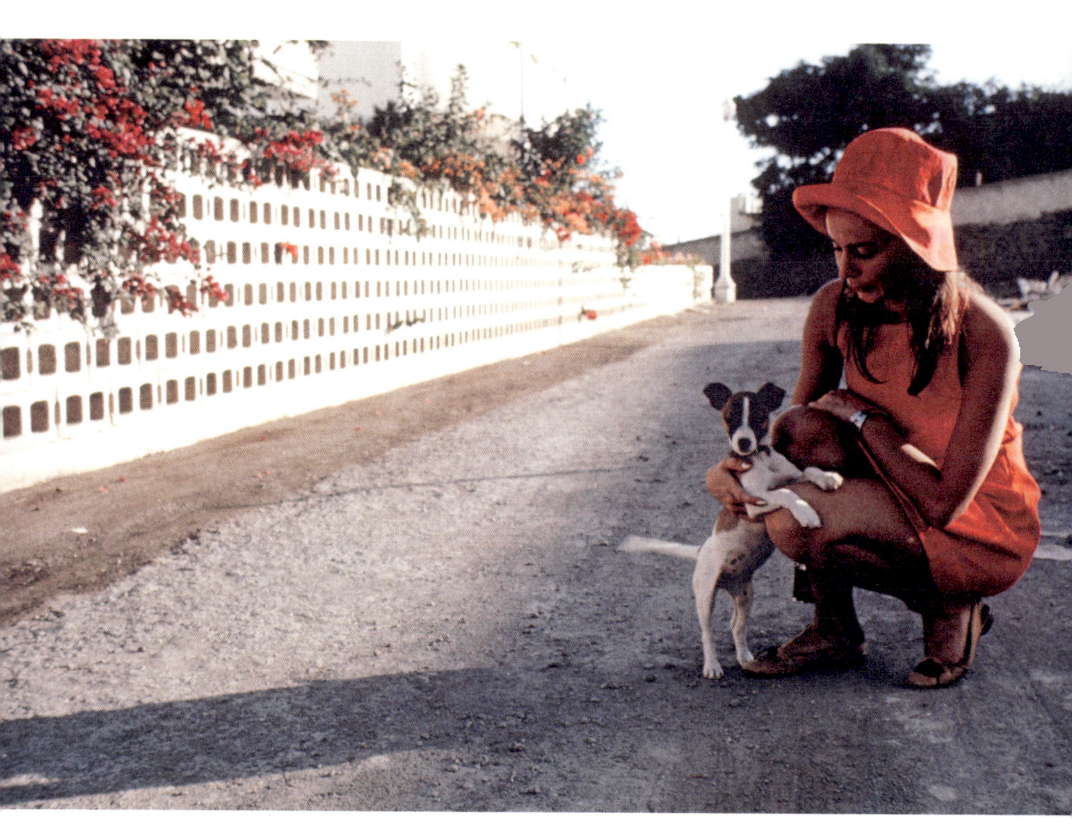

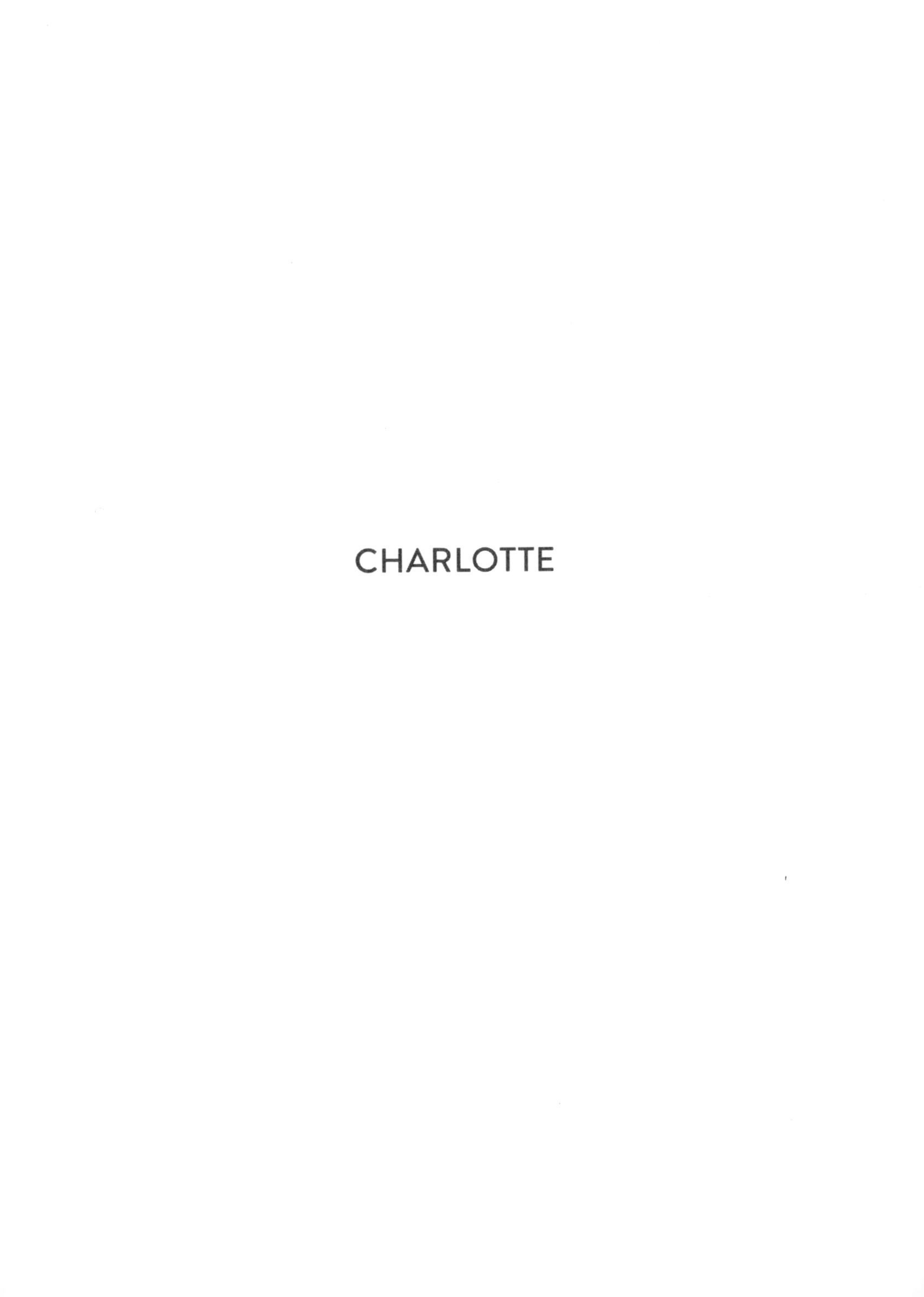

CHARLOTTE

Teneriffa, Nov '68

The slides are labelled
in an unfamiliar hand,
girlish and sloping.

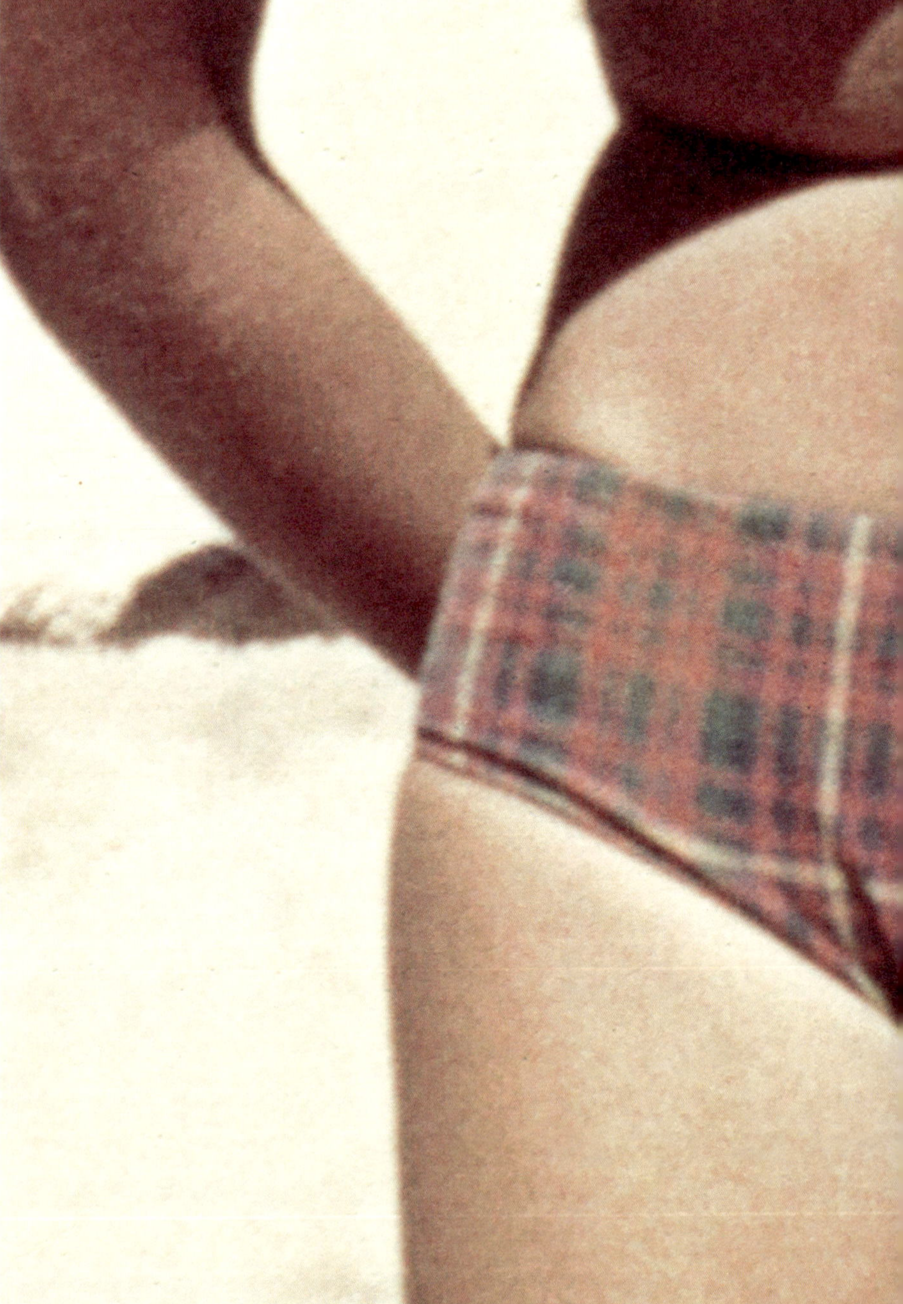

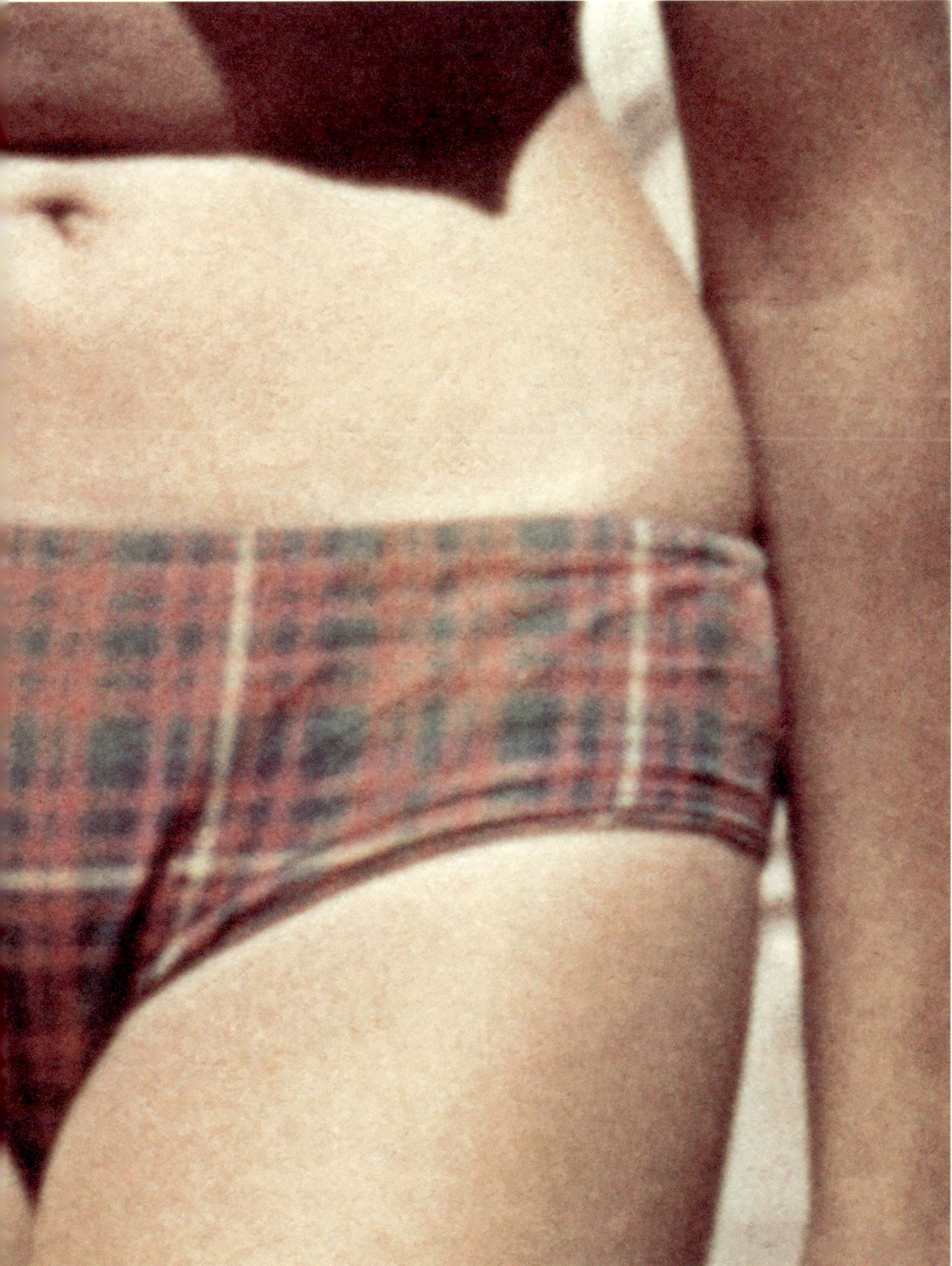

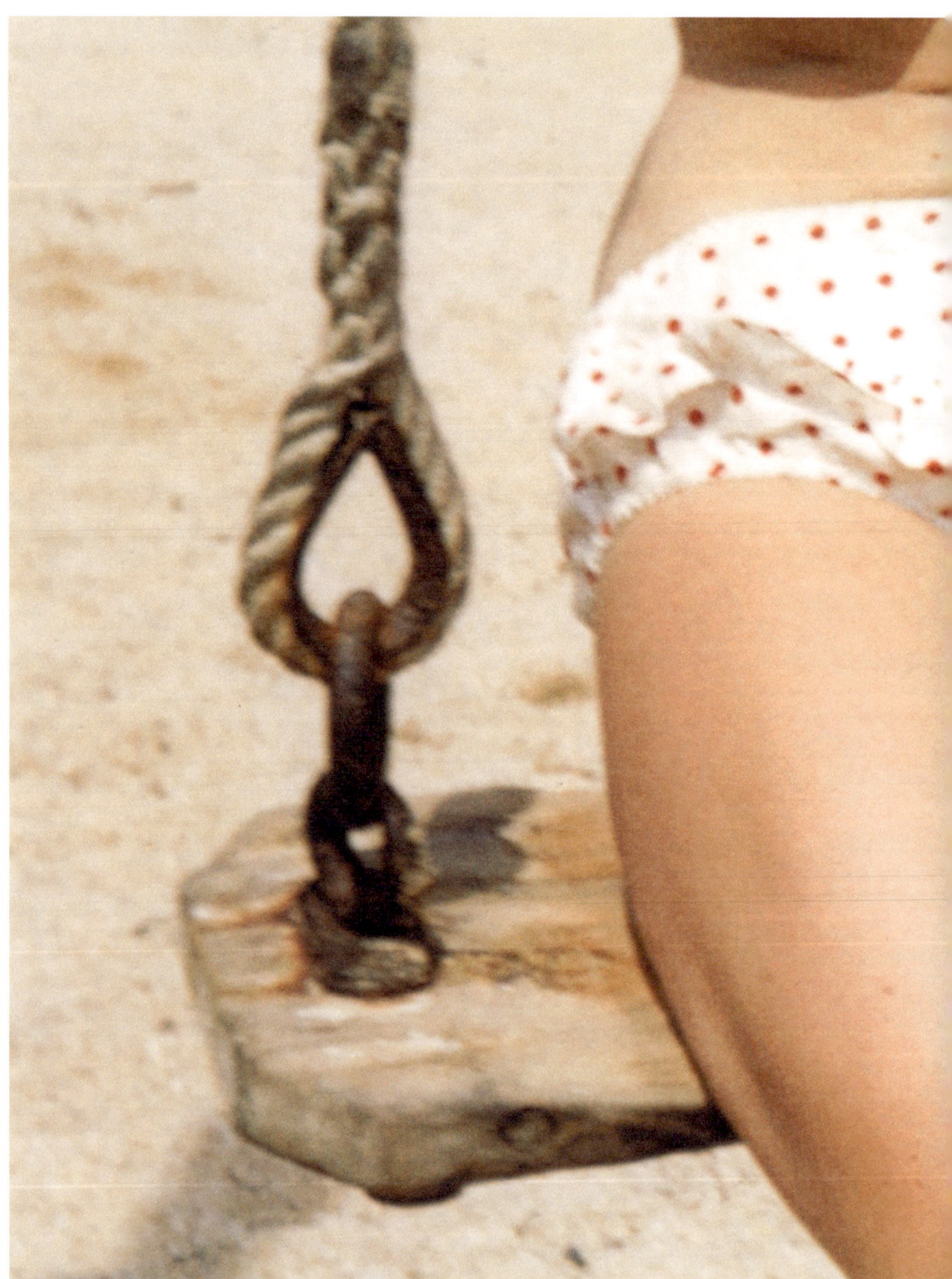

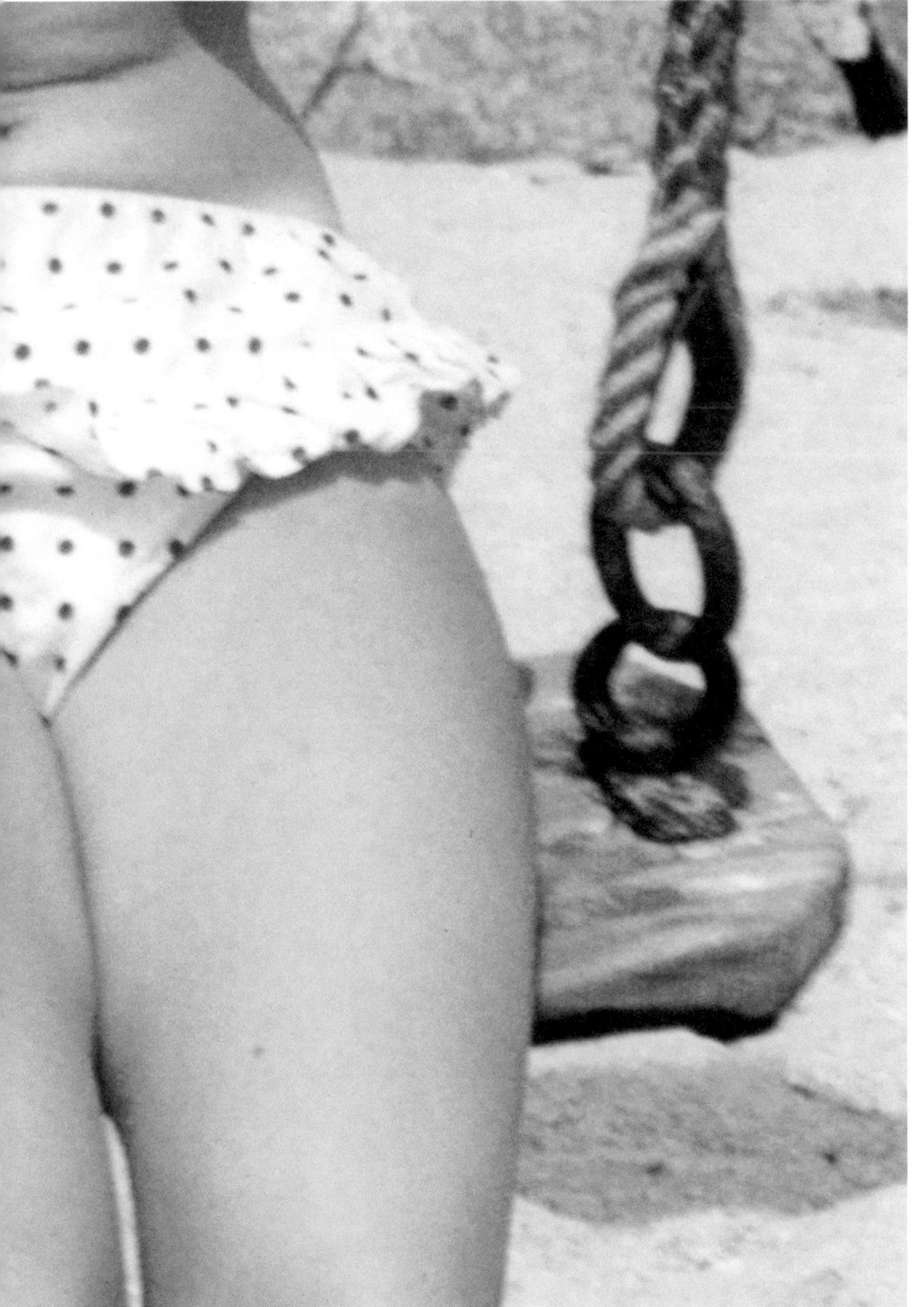

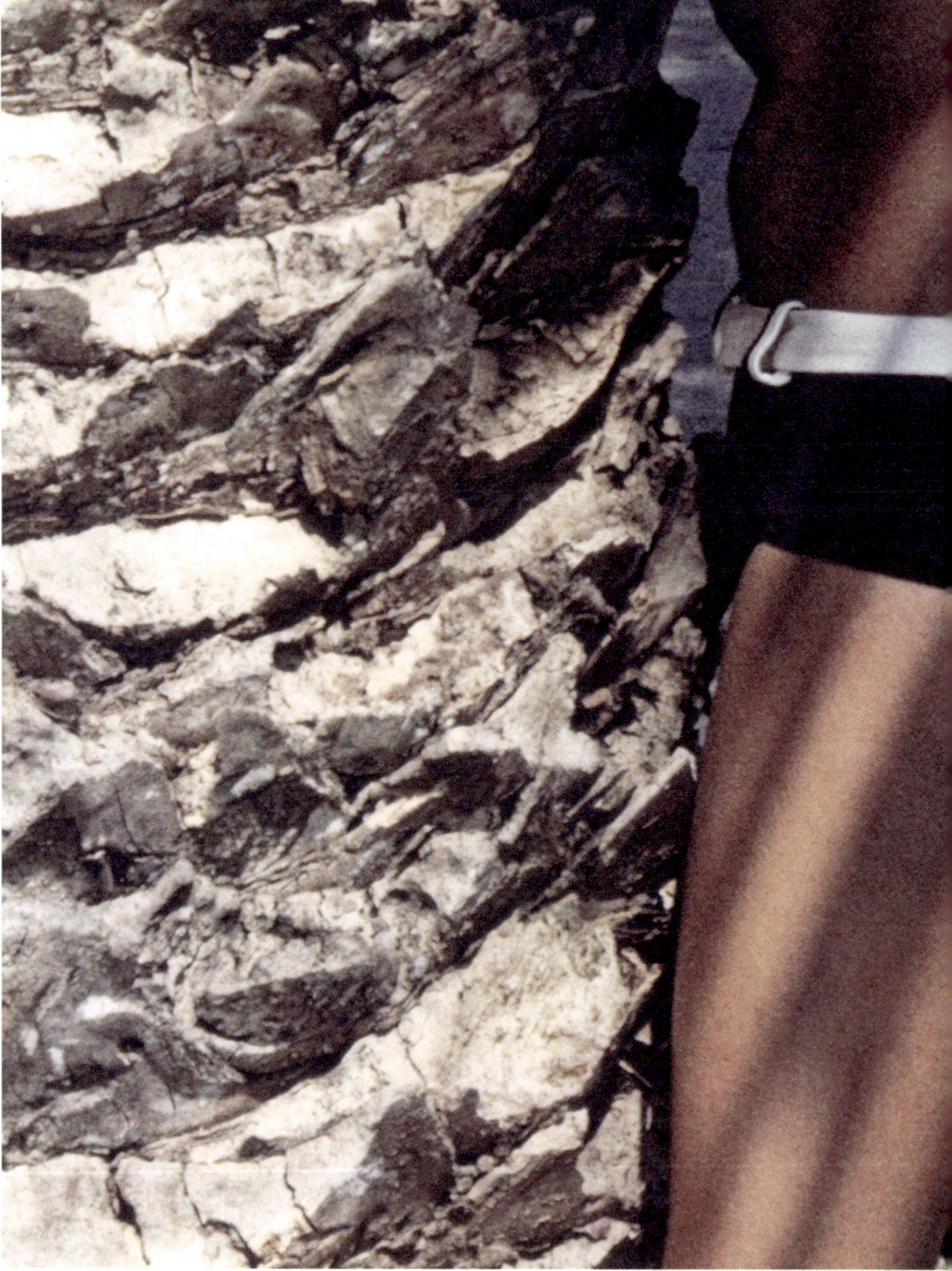

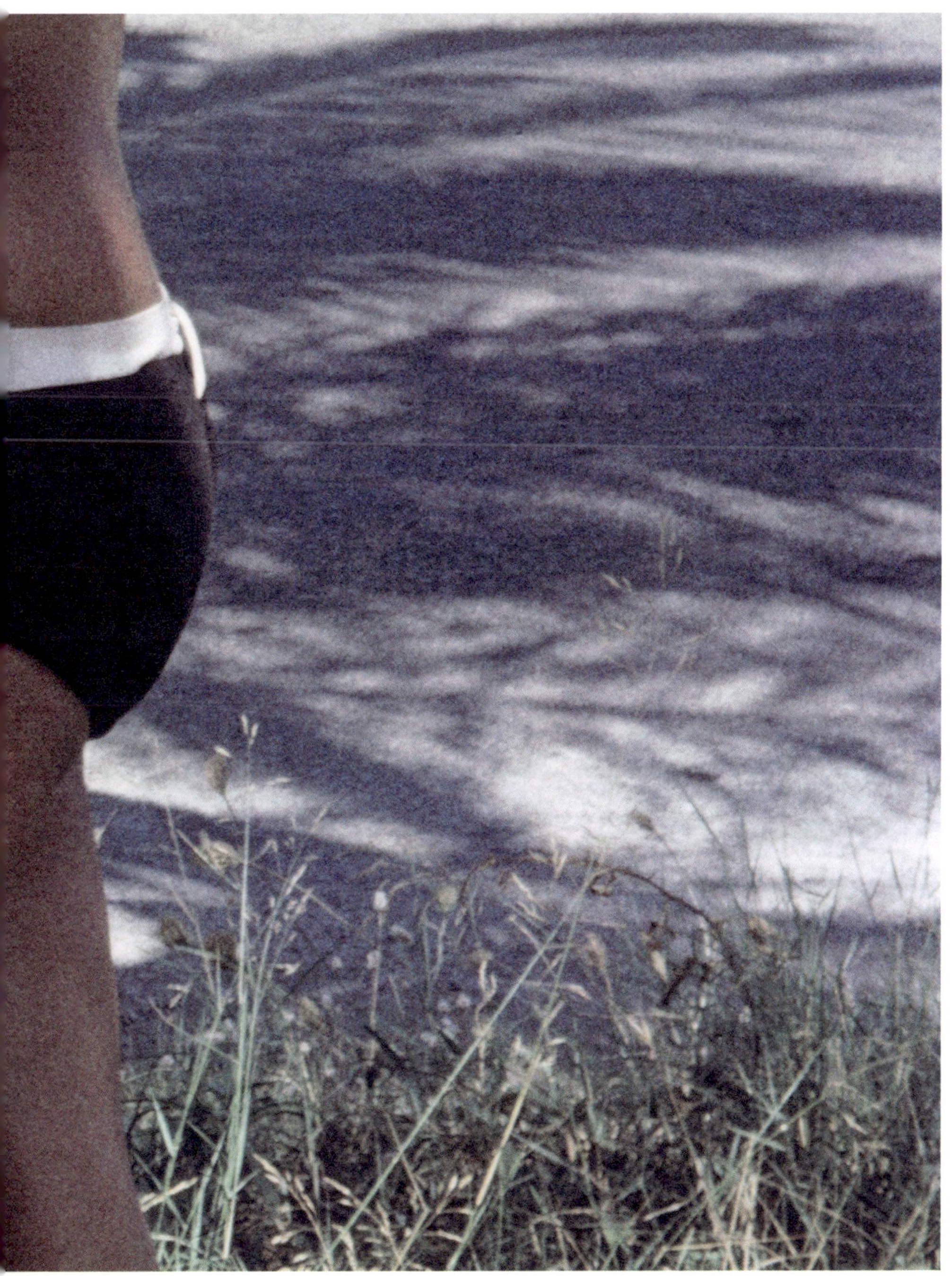

JUDY

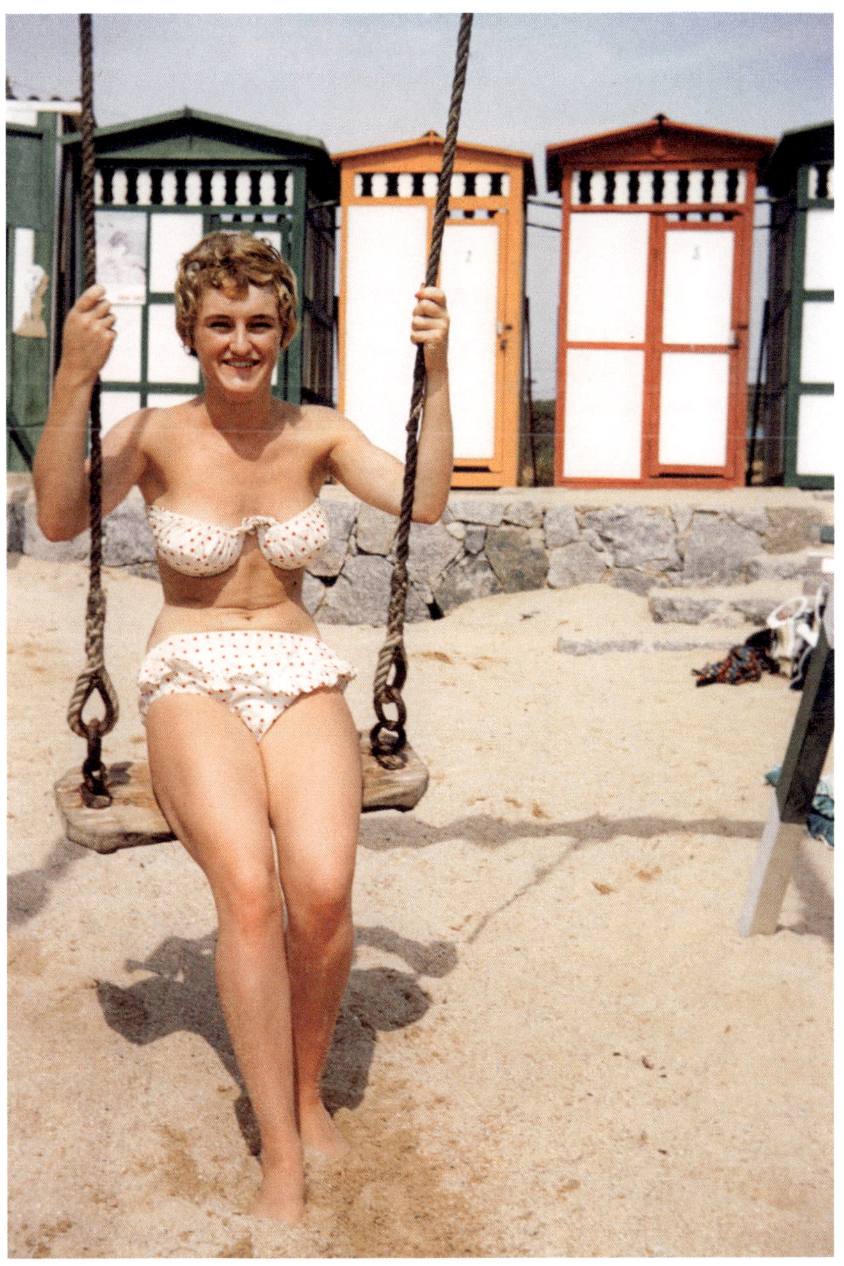

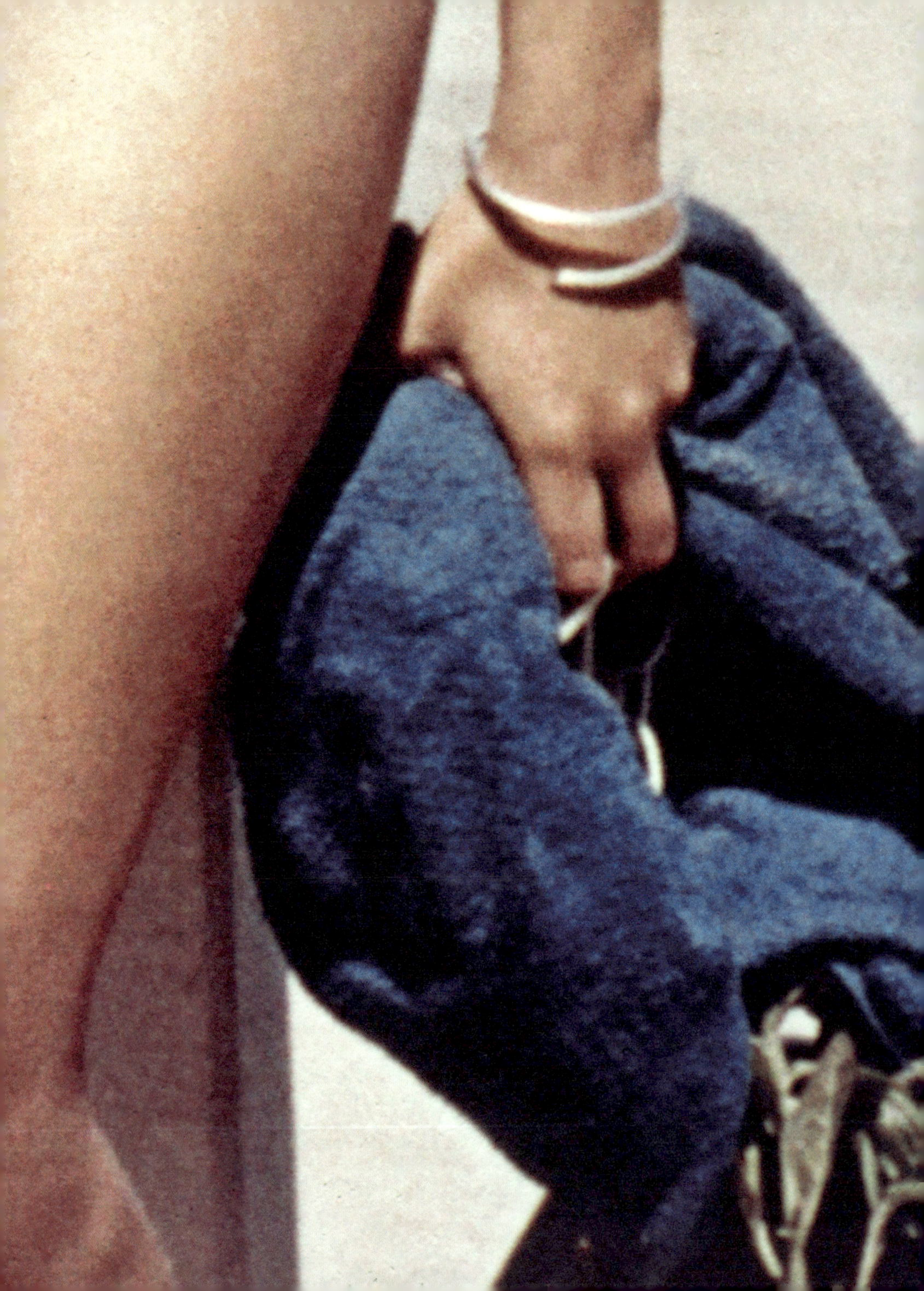

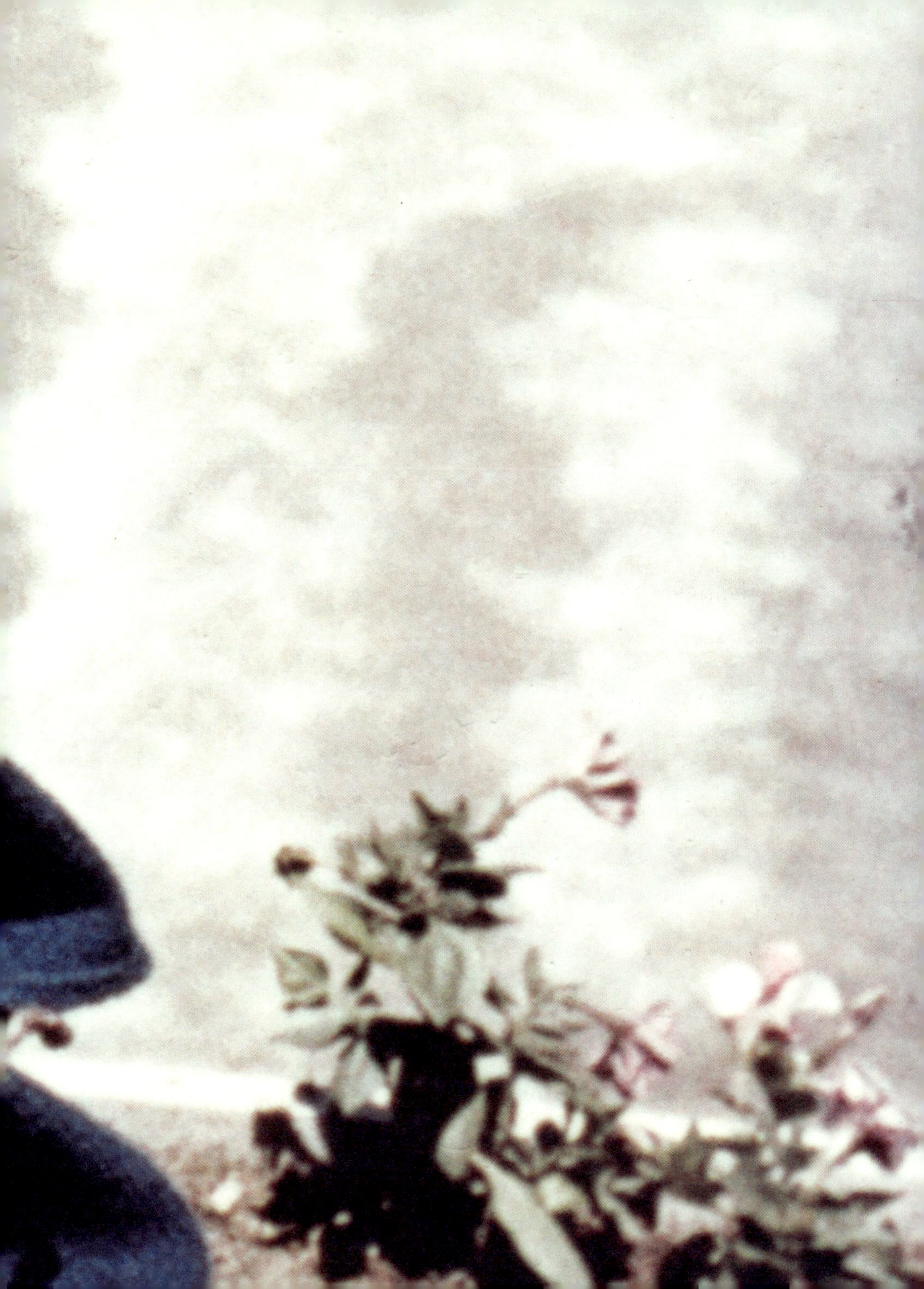

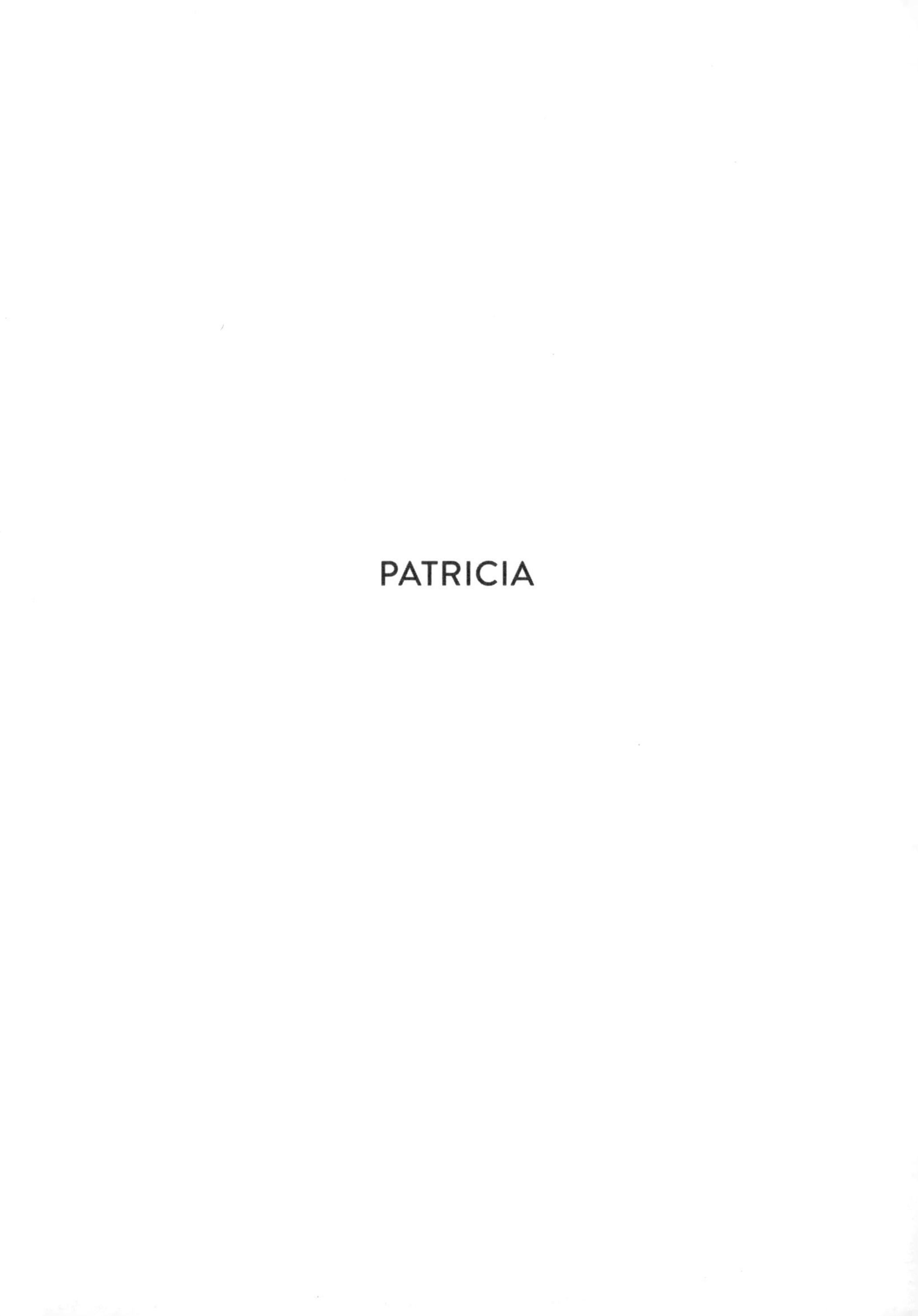

PATRICIA

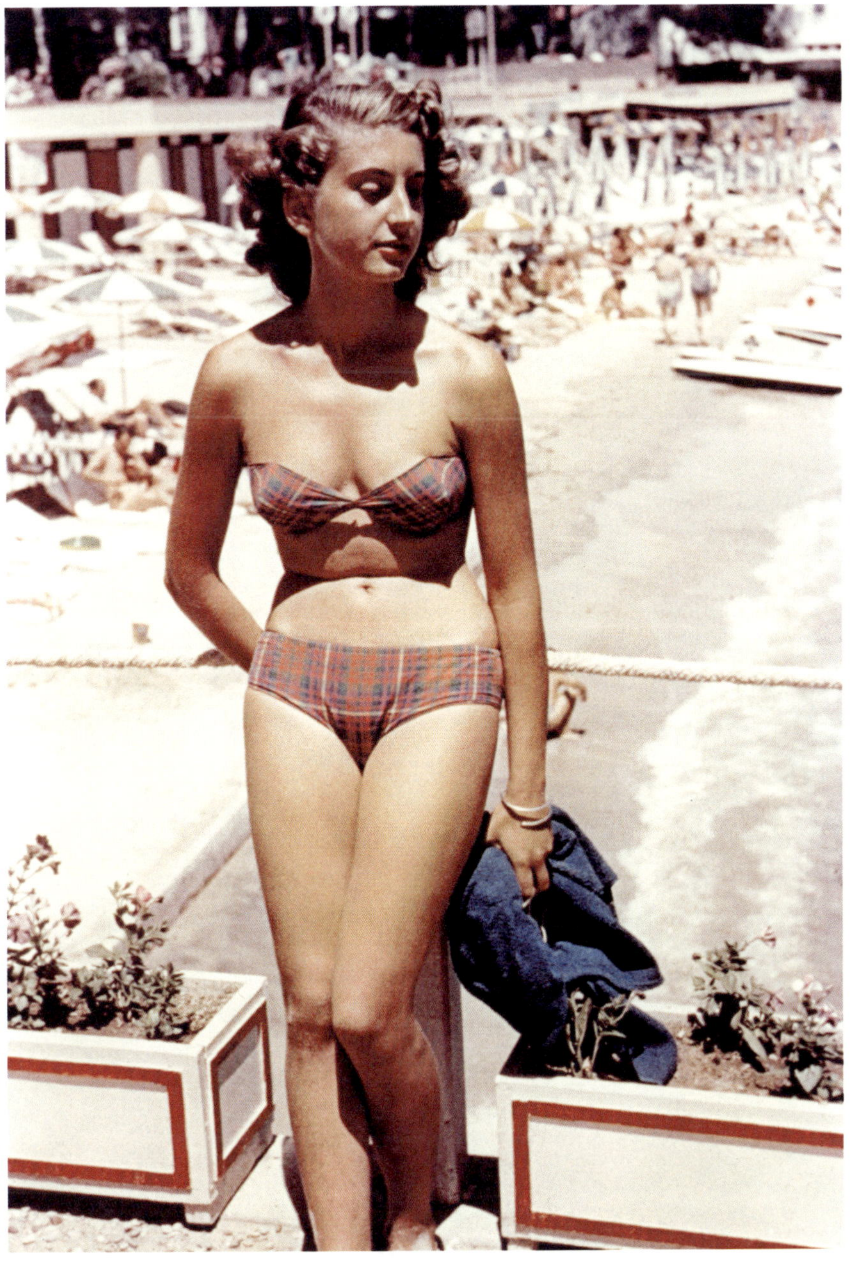

She could be on set.

Perhaps they met on the
Promenade des Anglais.
(He kept her letters in a box.)

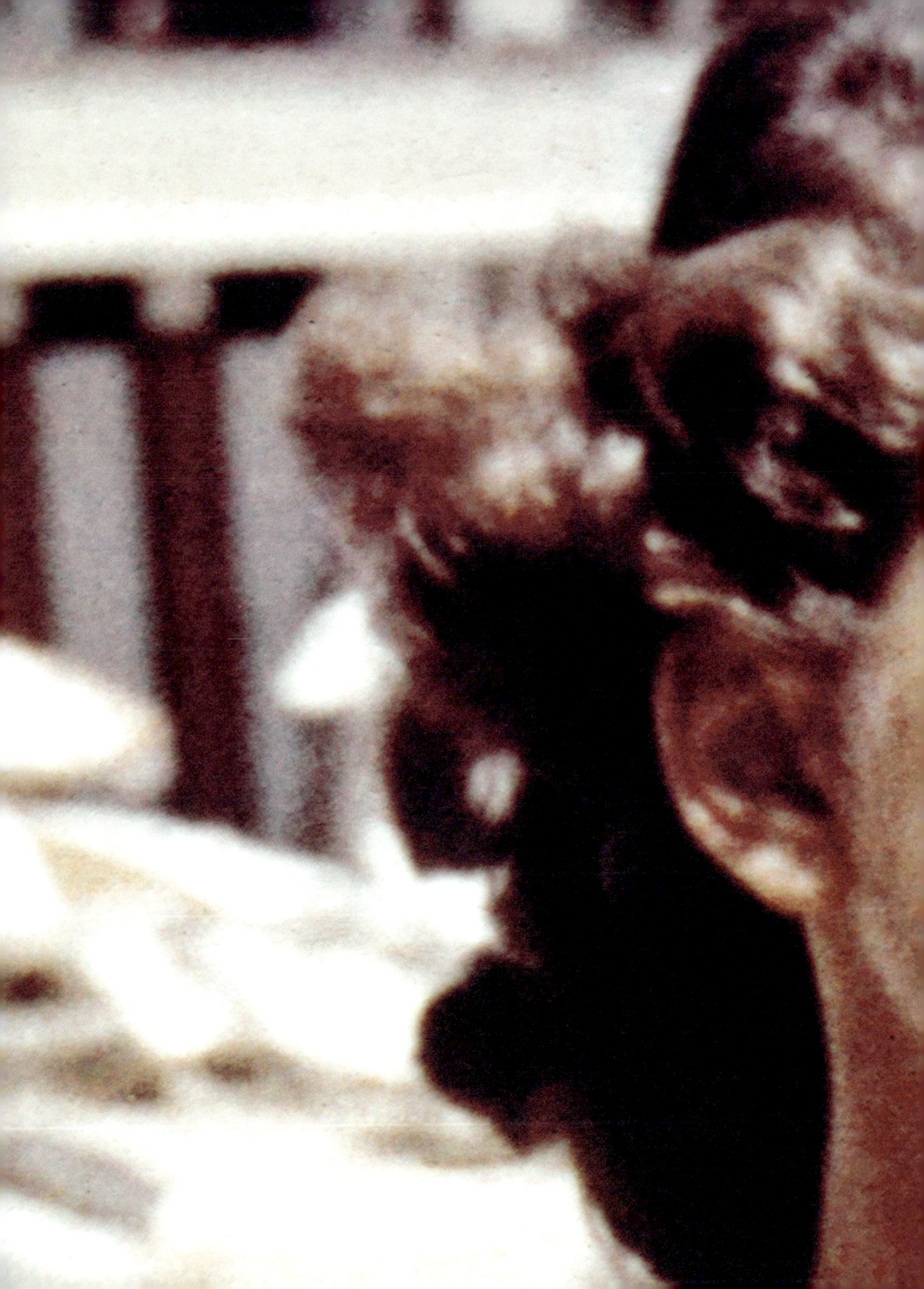

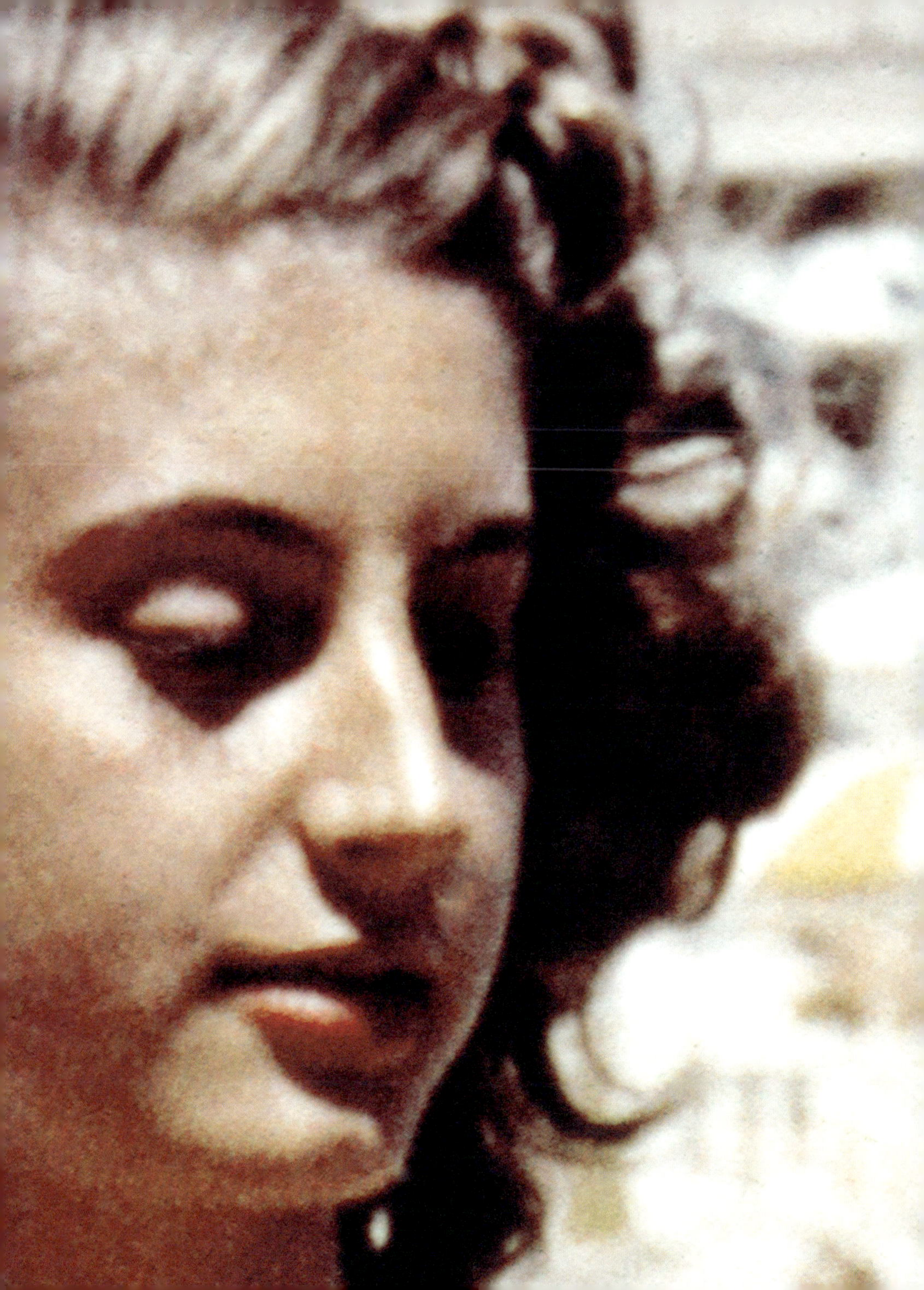

A torn-out note on lined paper,
blue ink, distinctively French handwriting.
Send me the photos you took on the beach!

(He has recently returned from National
Service with his Zeiss Ikon.)

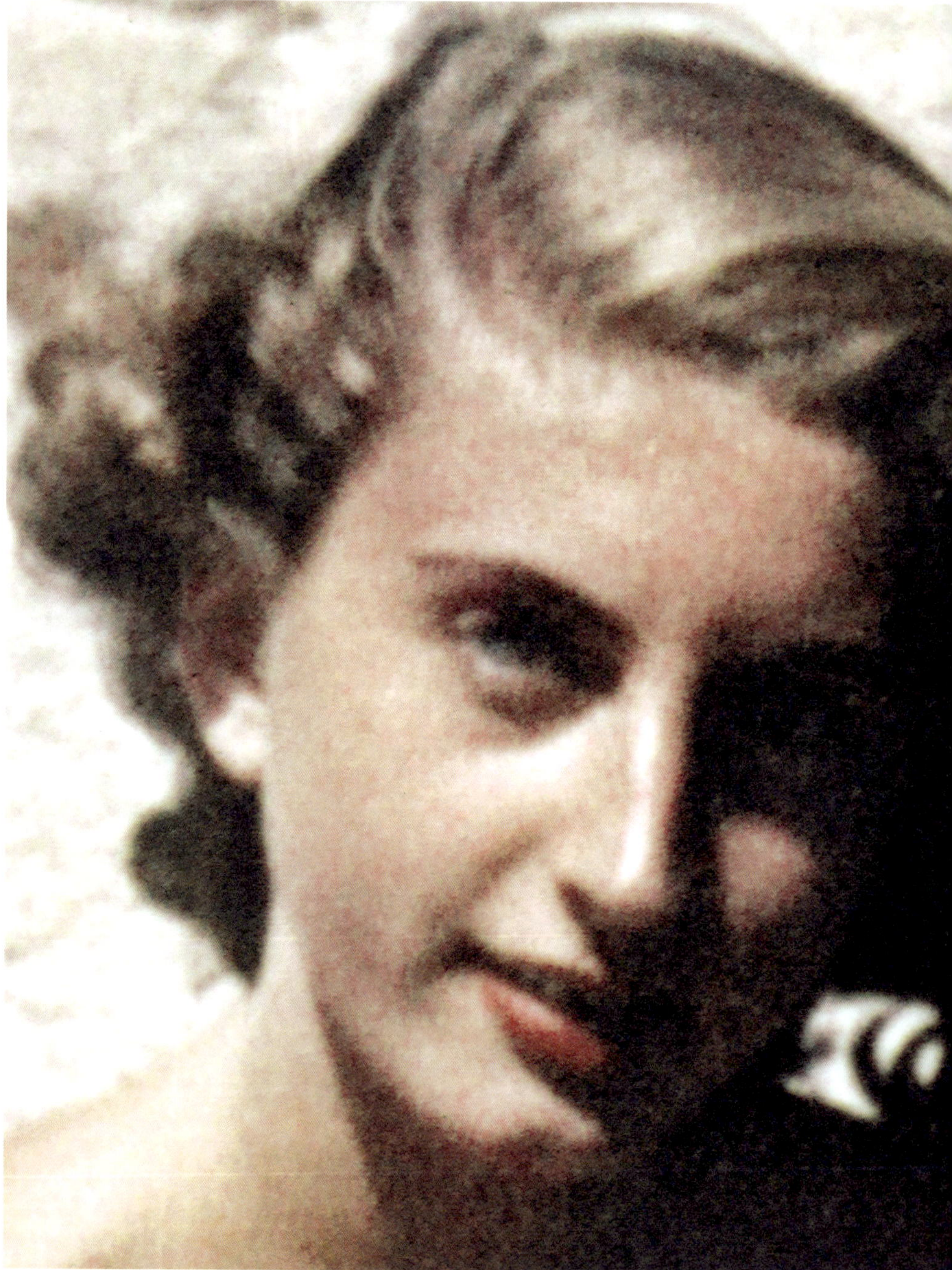

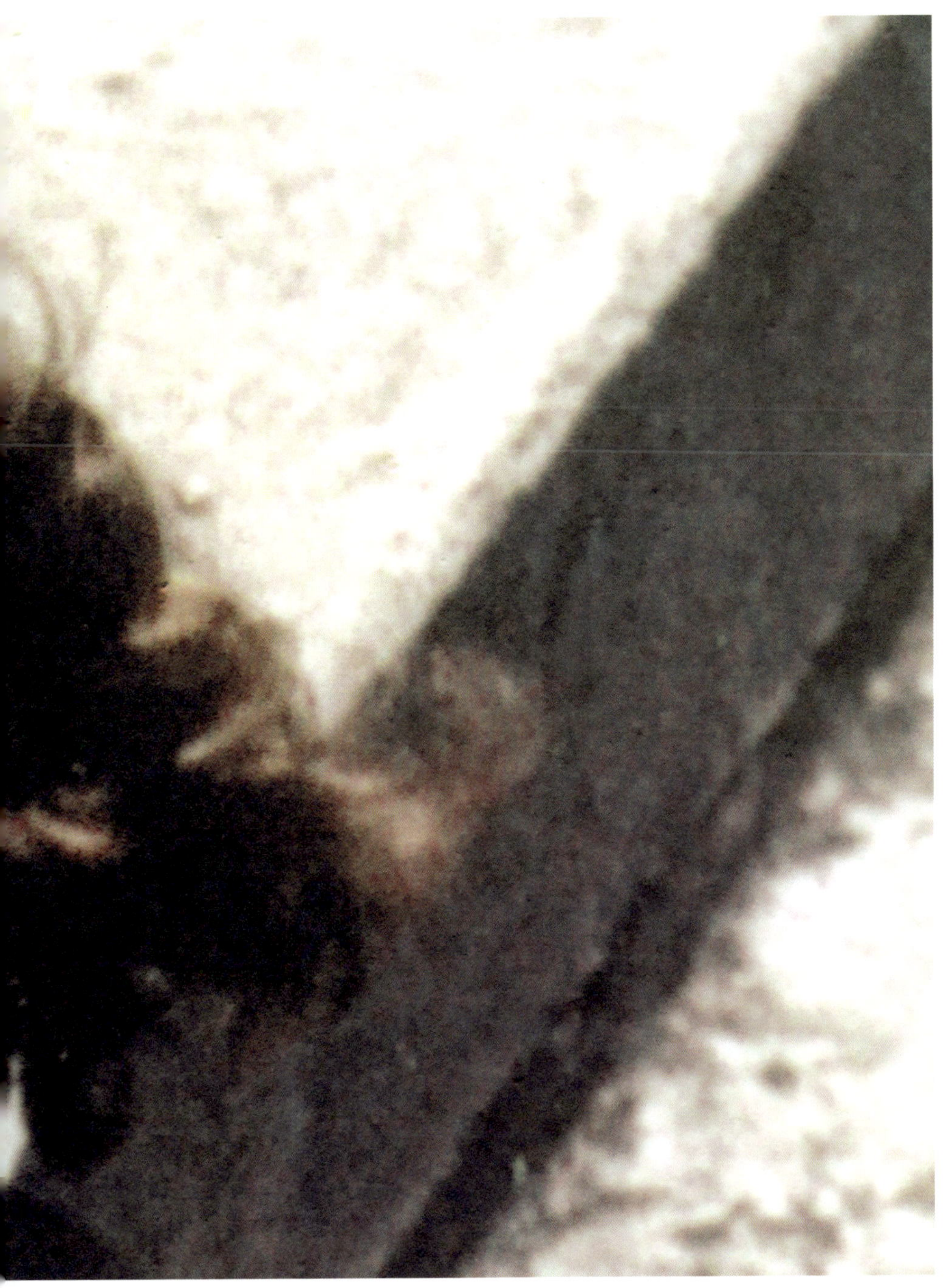

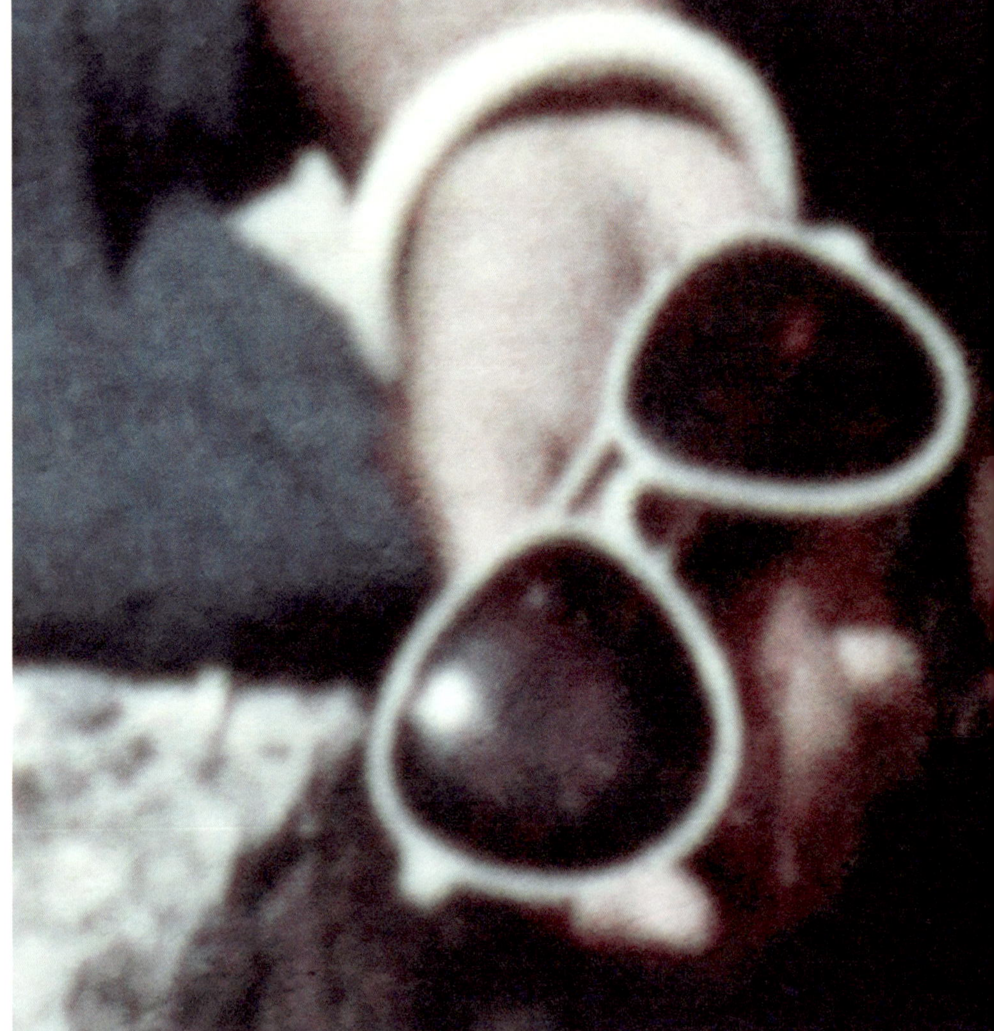

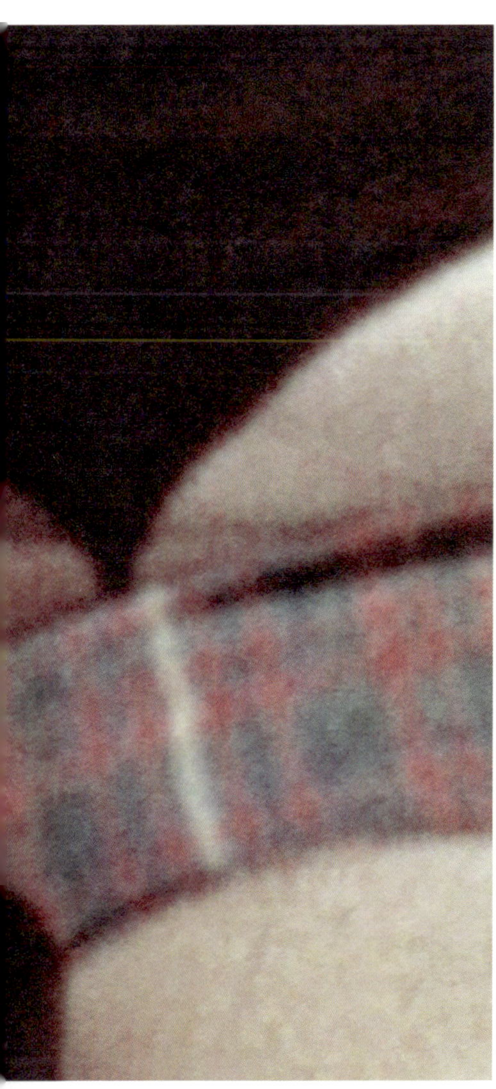

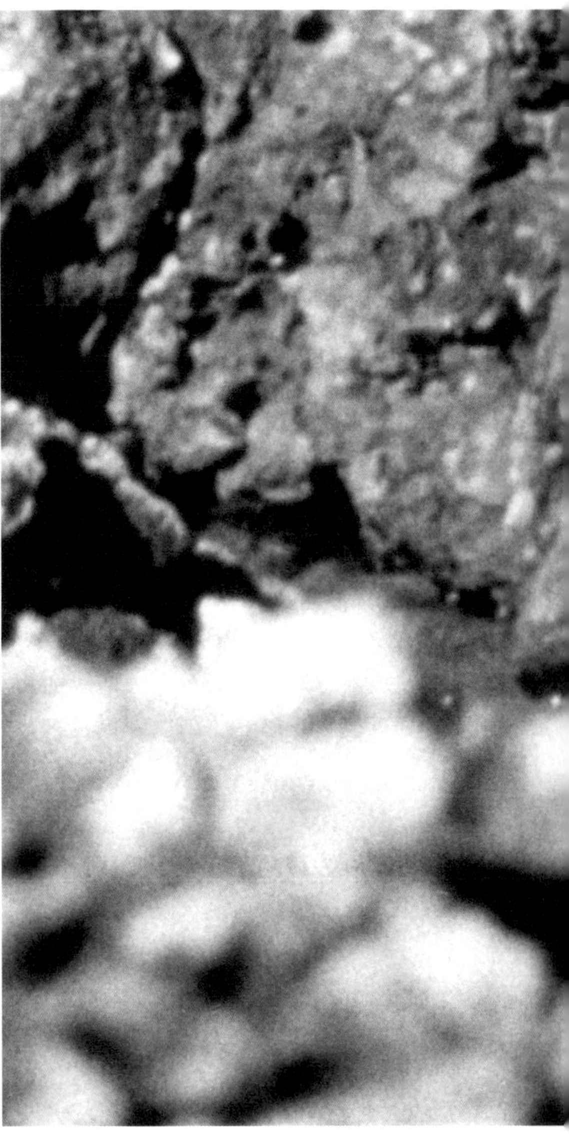

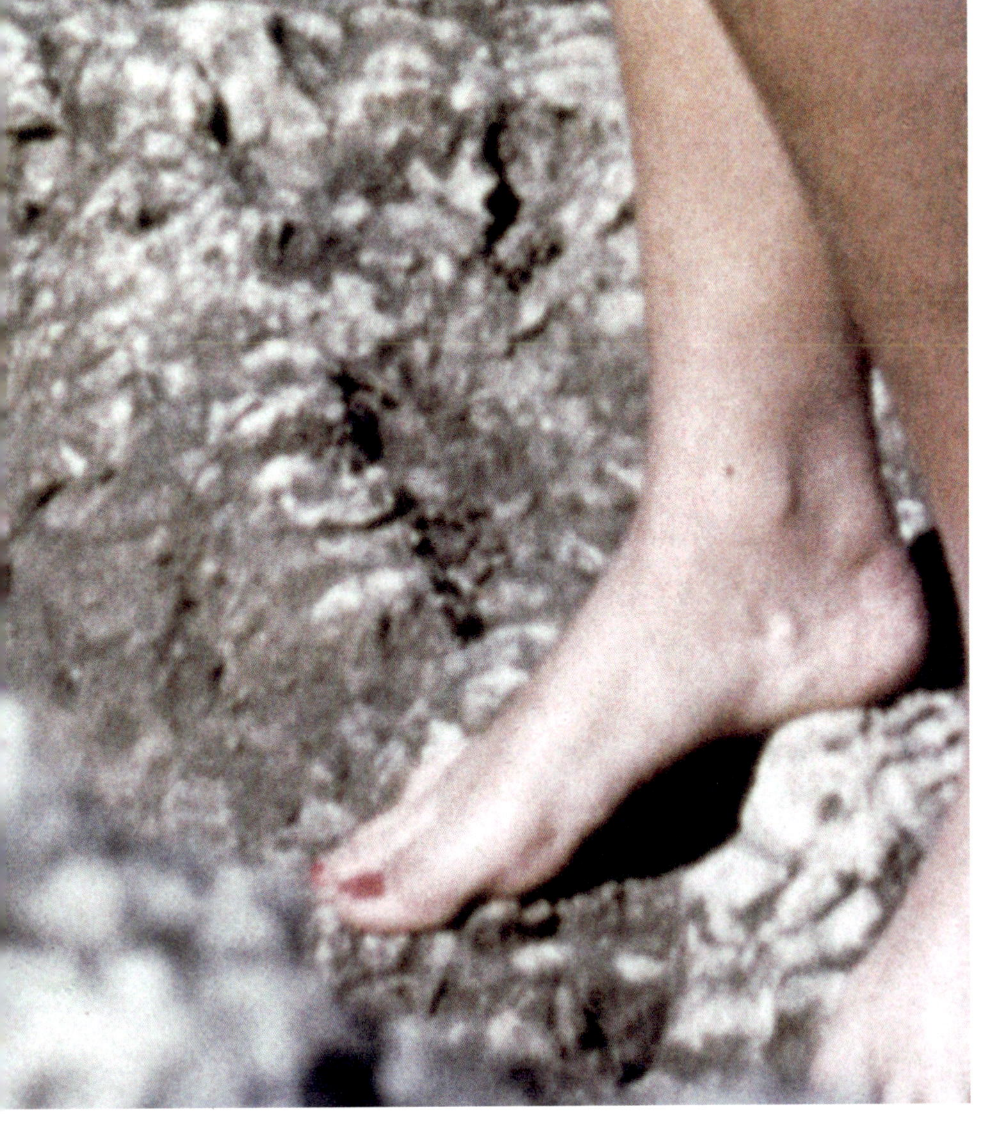

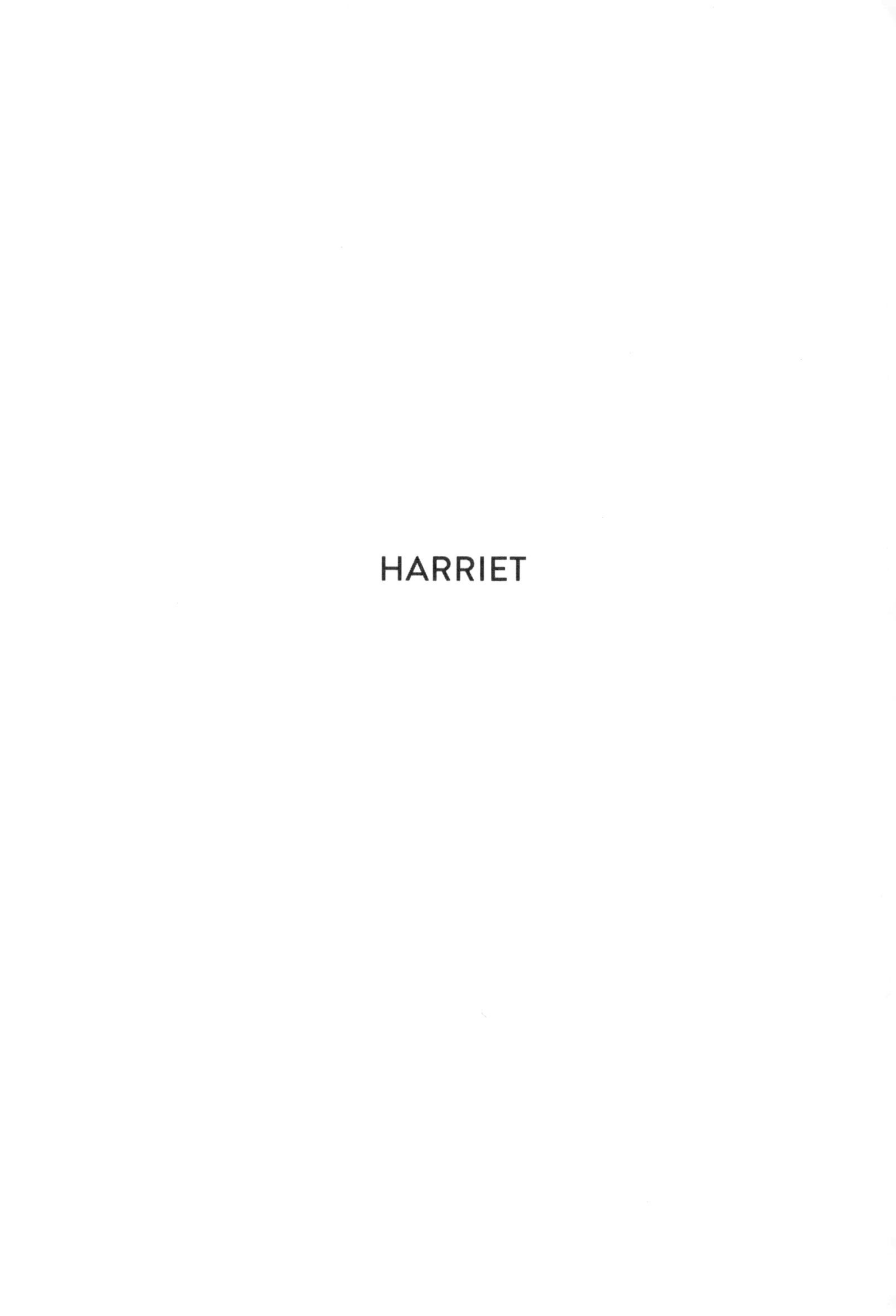

HARRIET

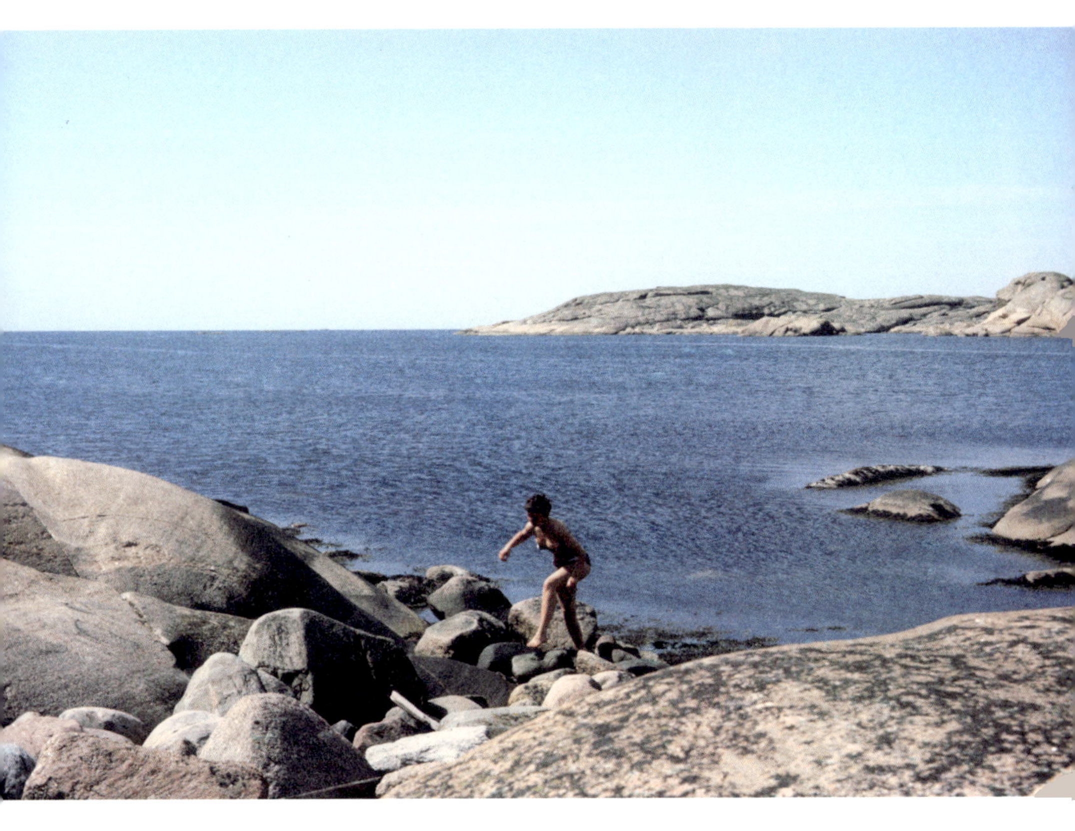

Sailing to Hallands Väderö
with my grandfather's friend Pelle.

The boat smelled of mackerel and seaweed, and the journey made my grandmother sick.

PIA

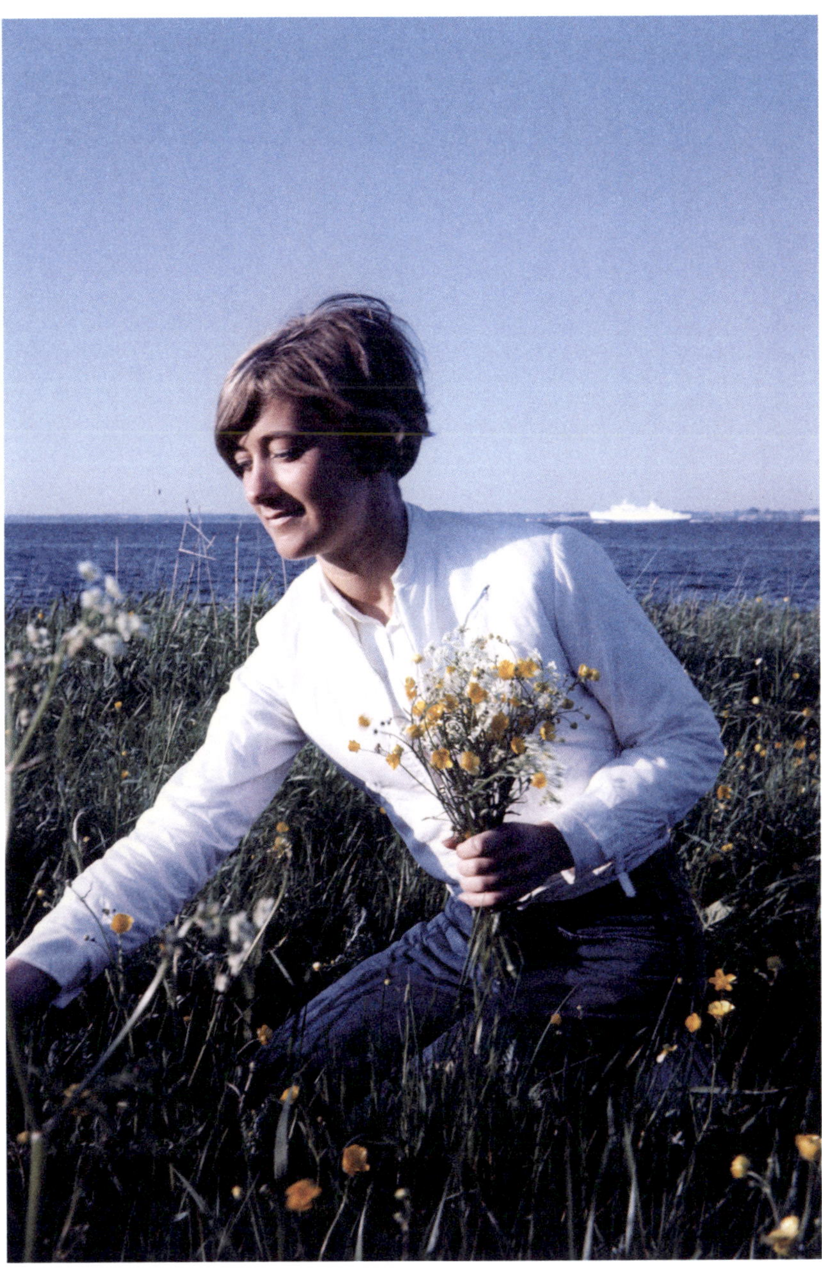

Look down at the flowers.
Towards me a bit.

Tears of frustration
as I endured having my
photo taken for Peter Pan.

It took forever.

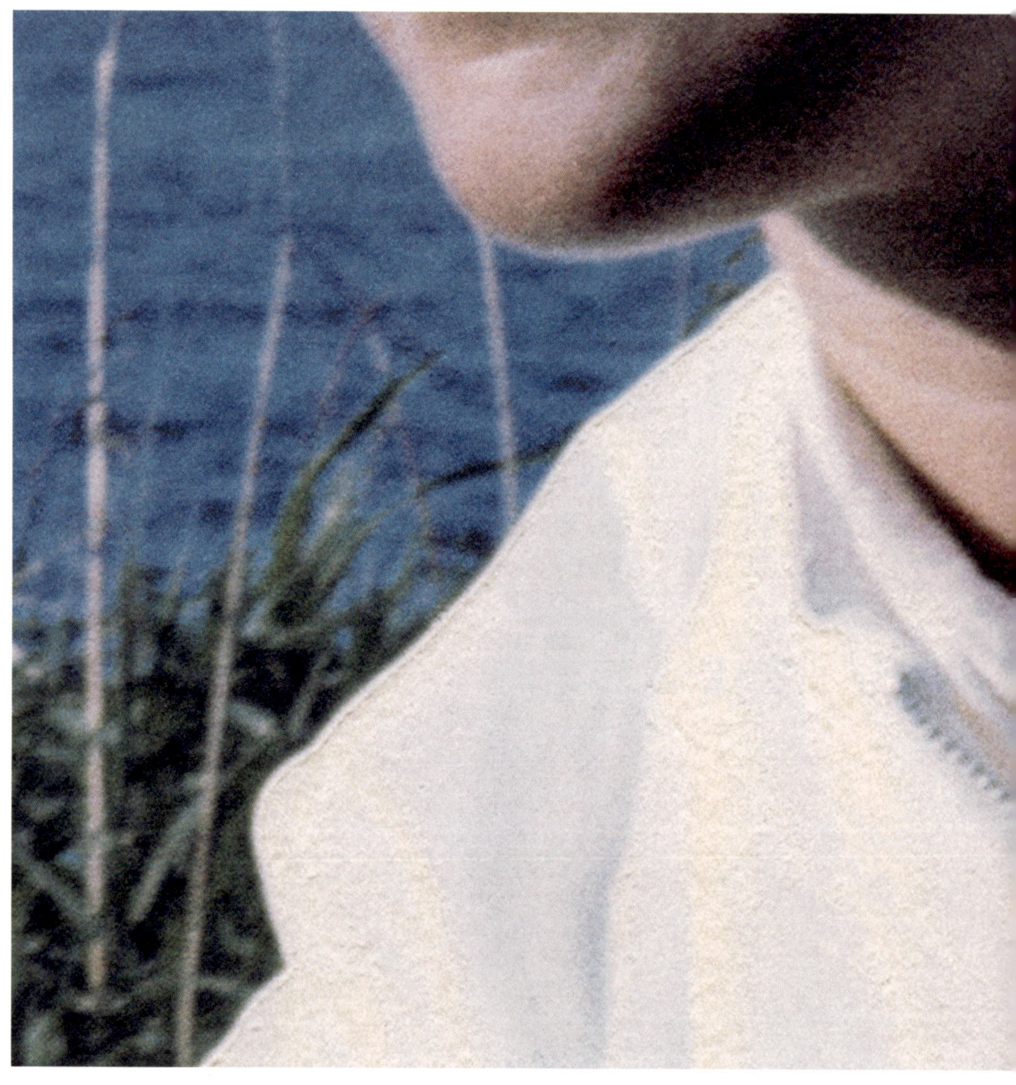

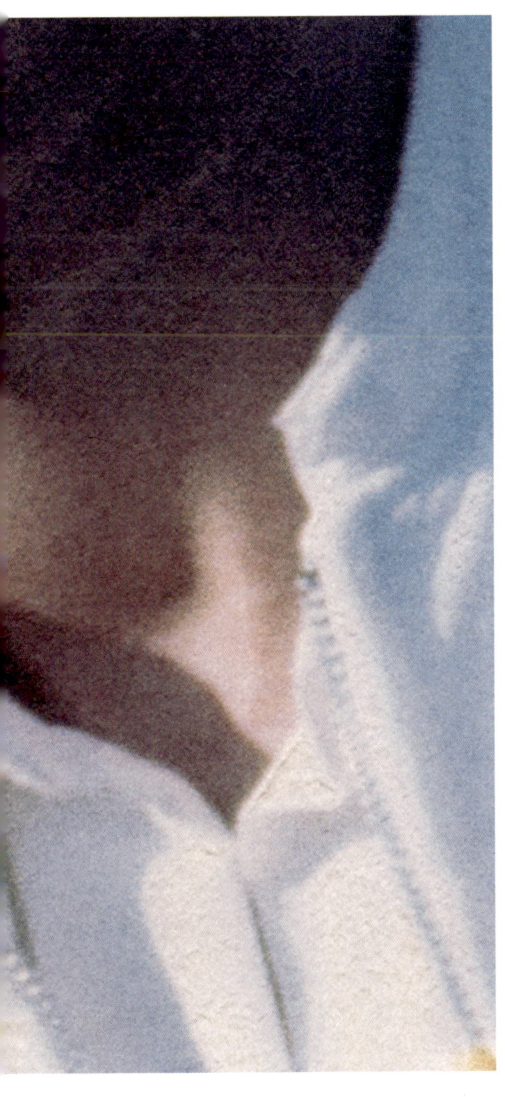

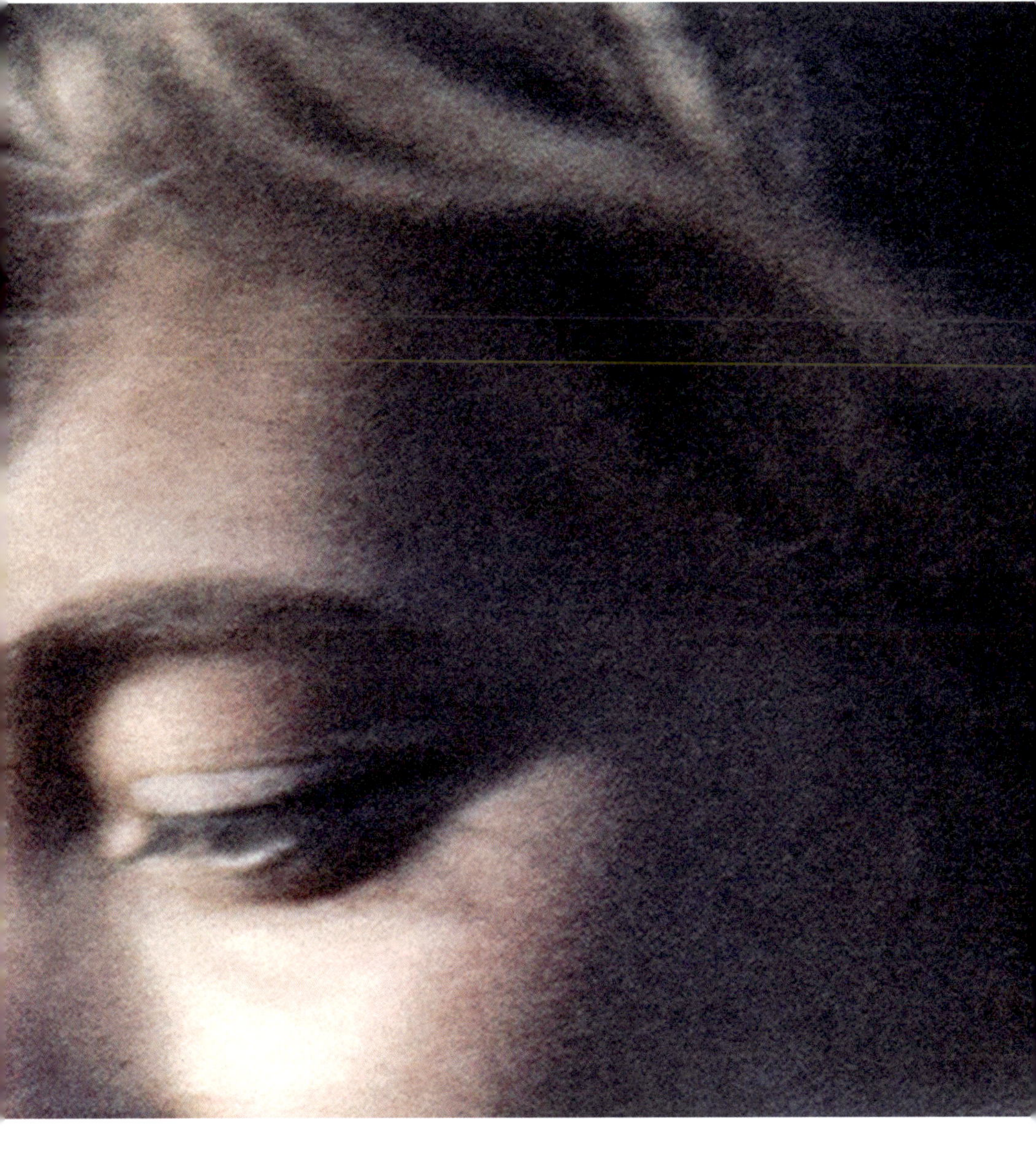

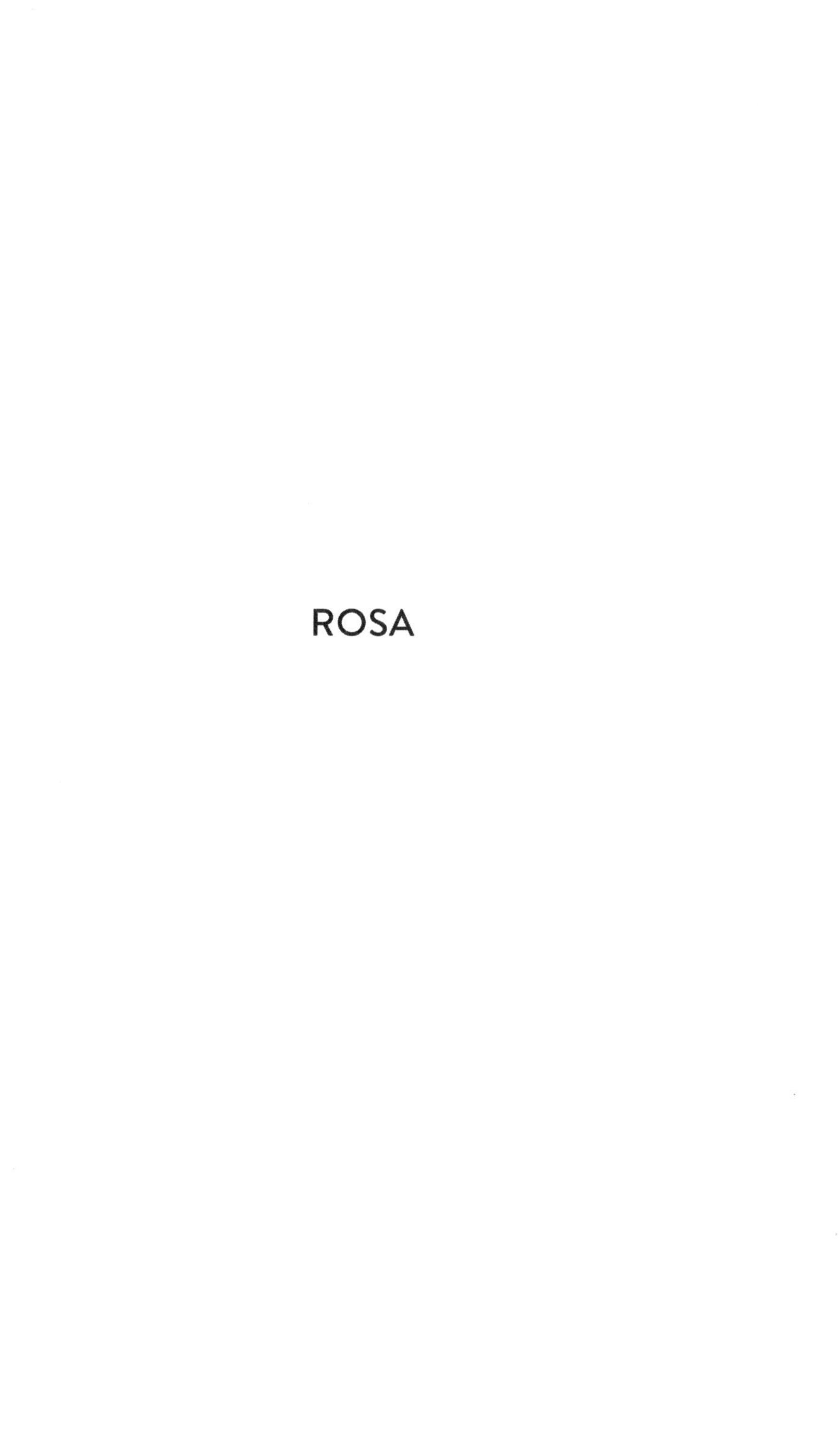

ROSA

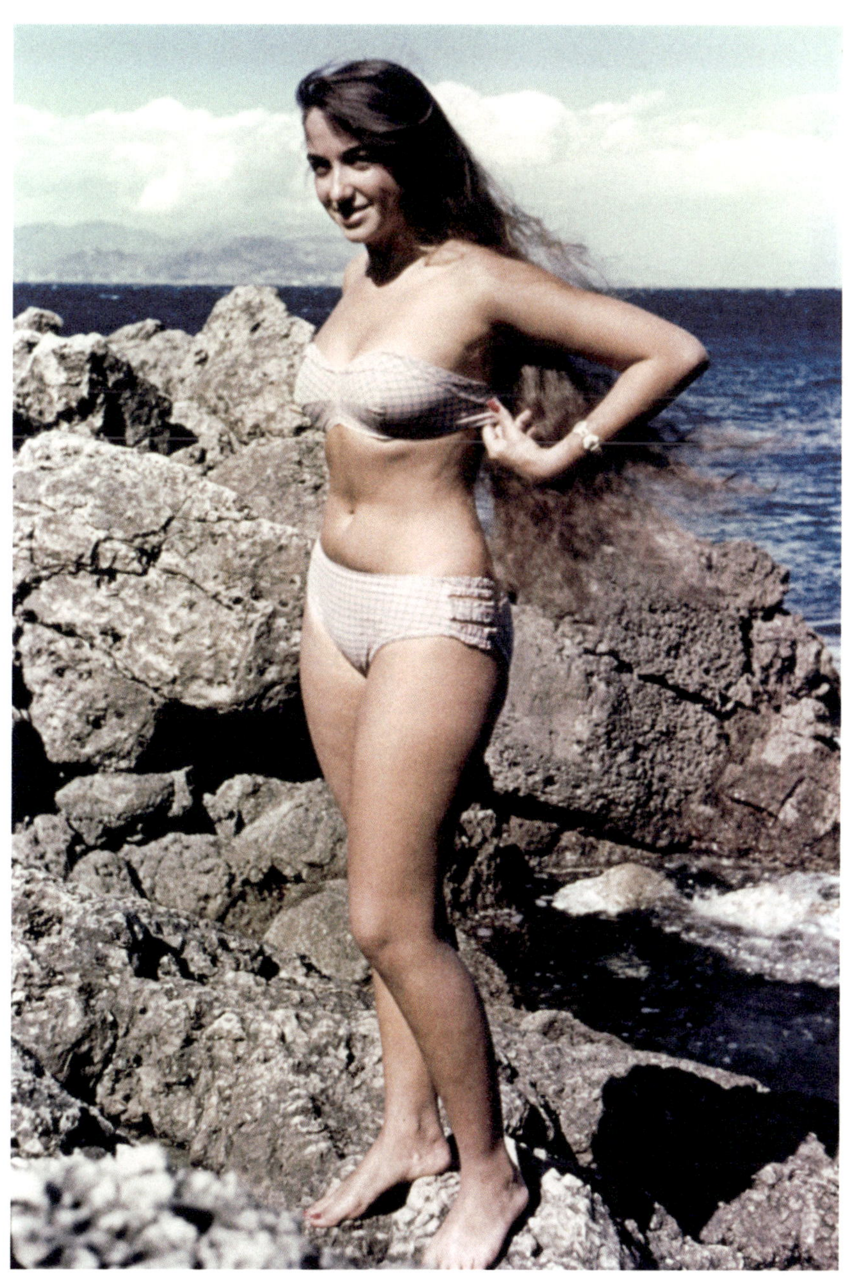

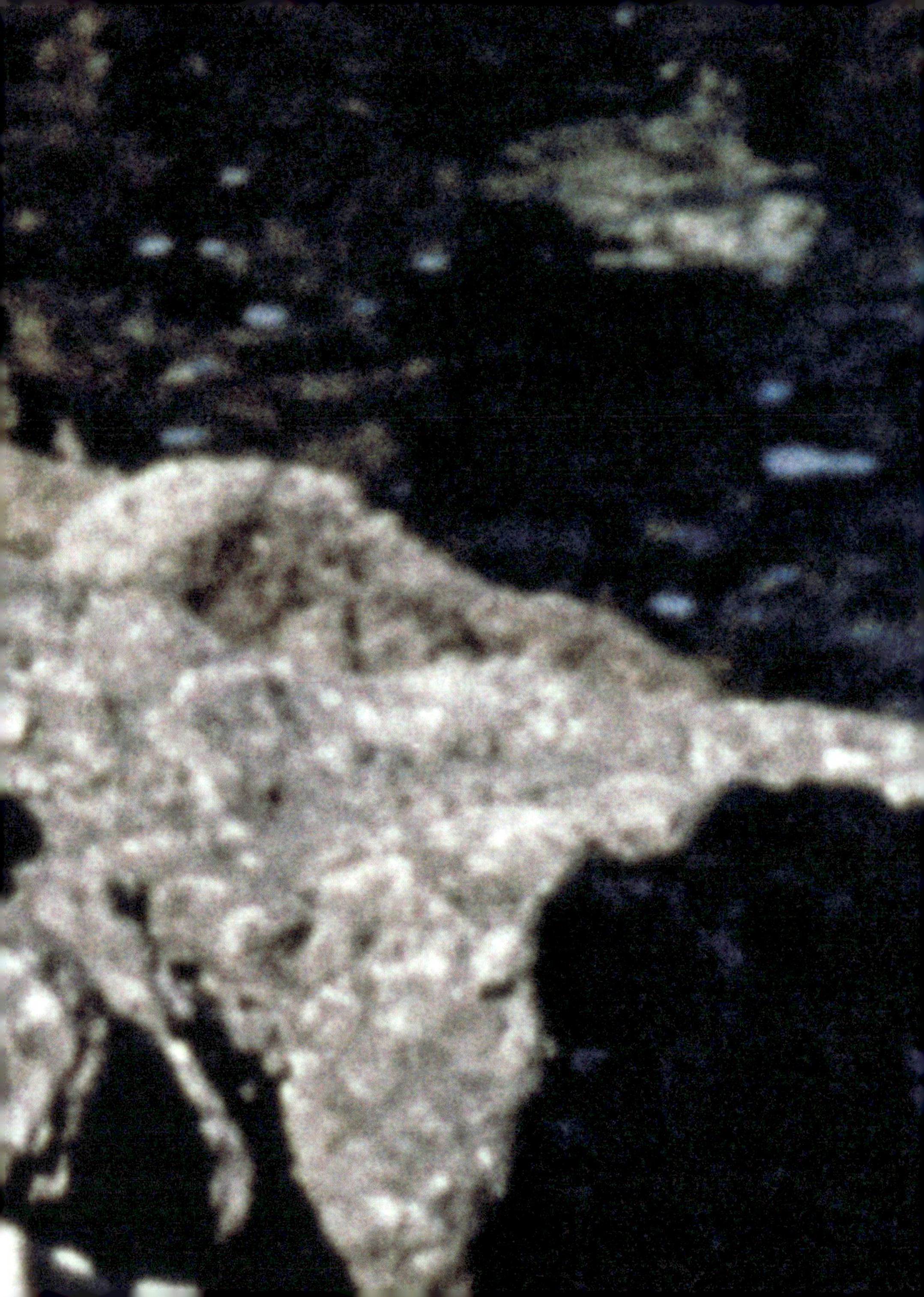

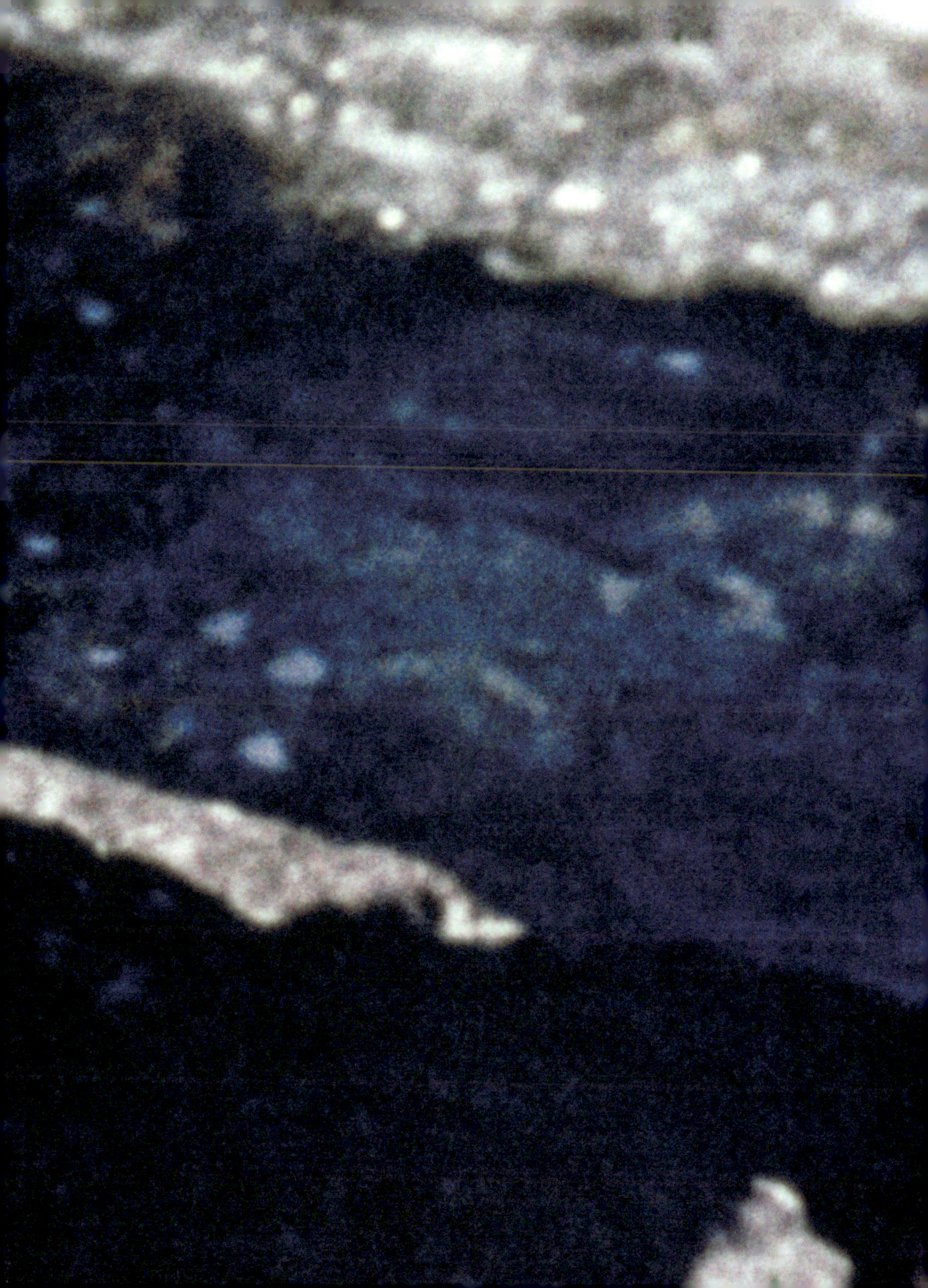

MAJA

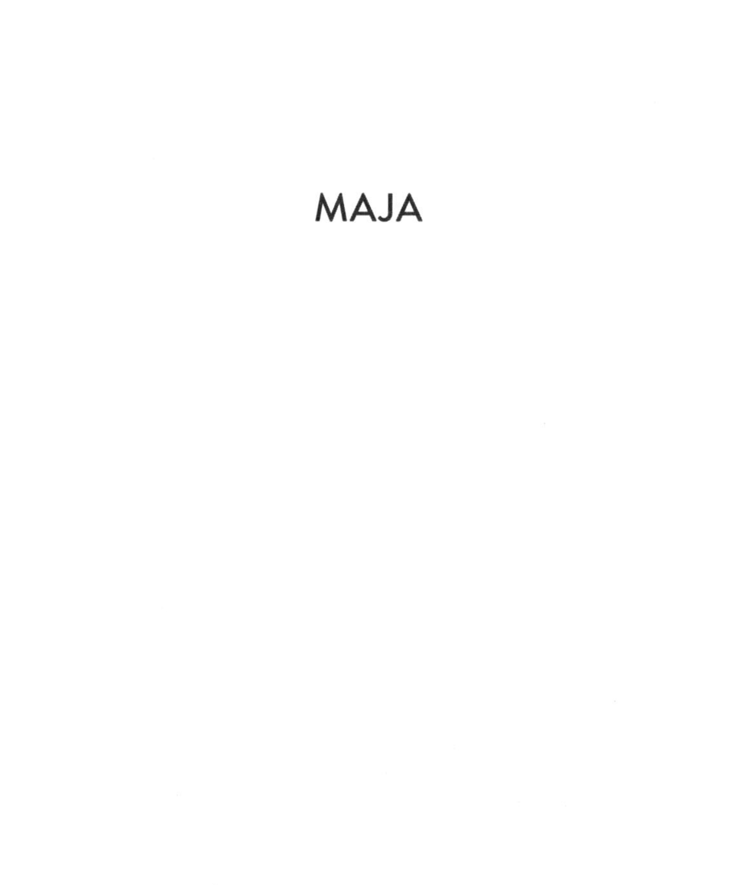

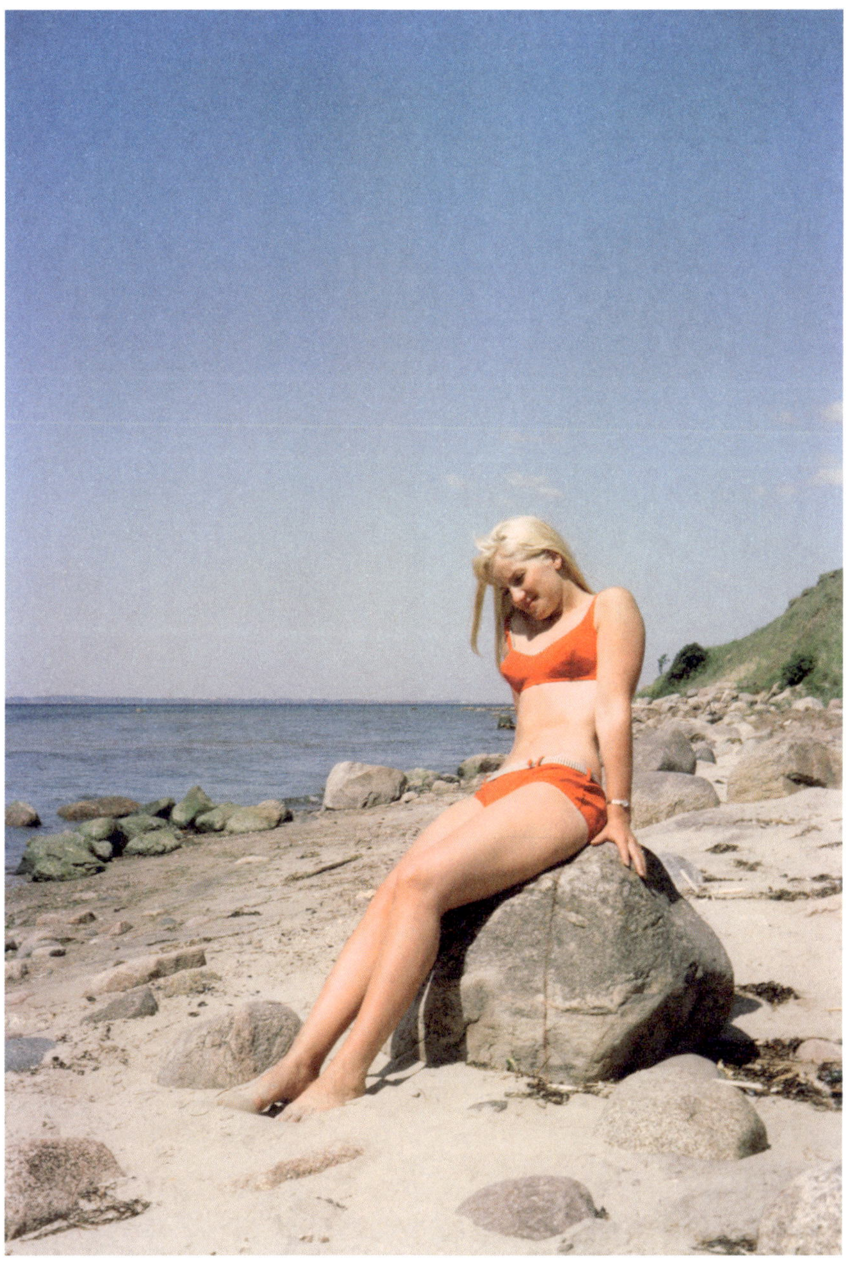

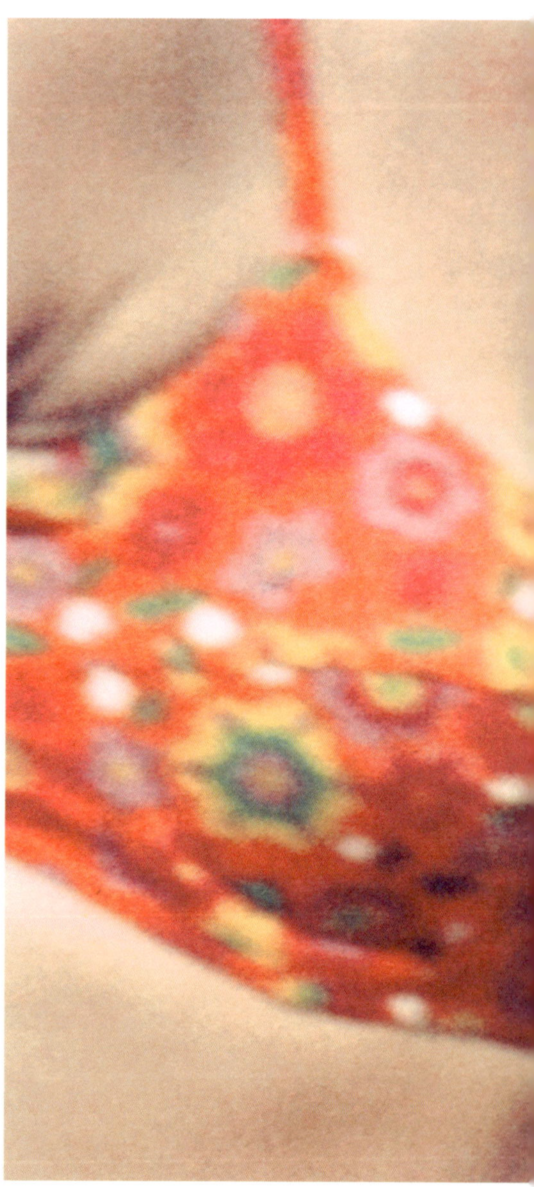

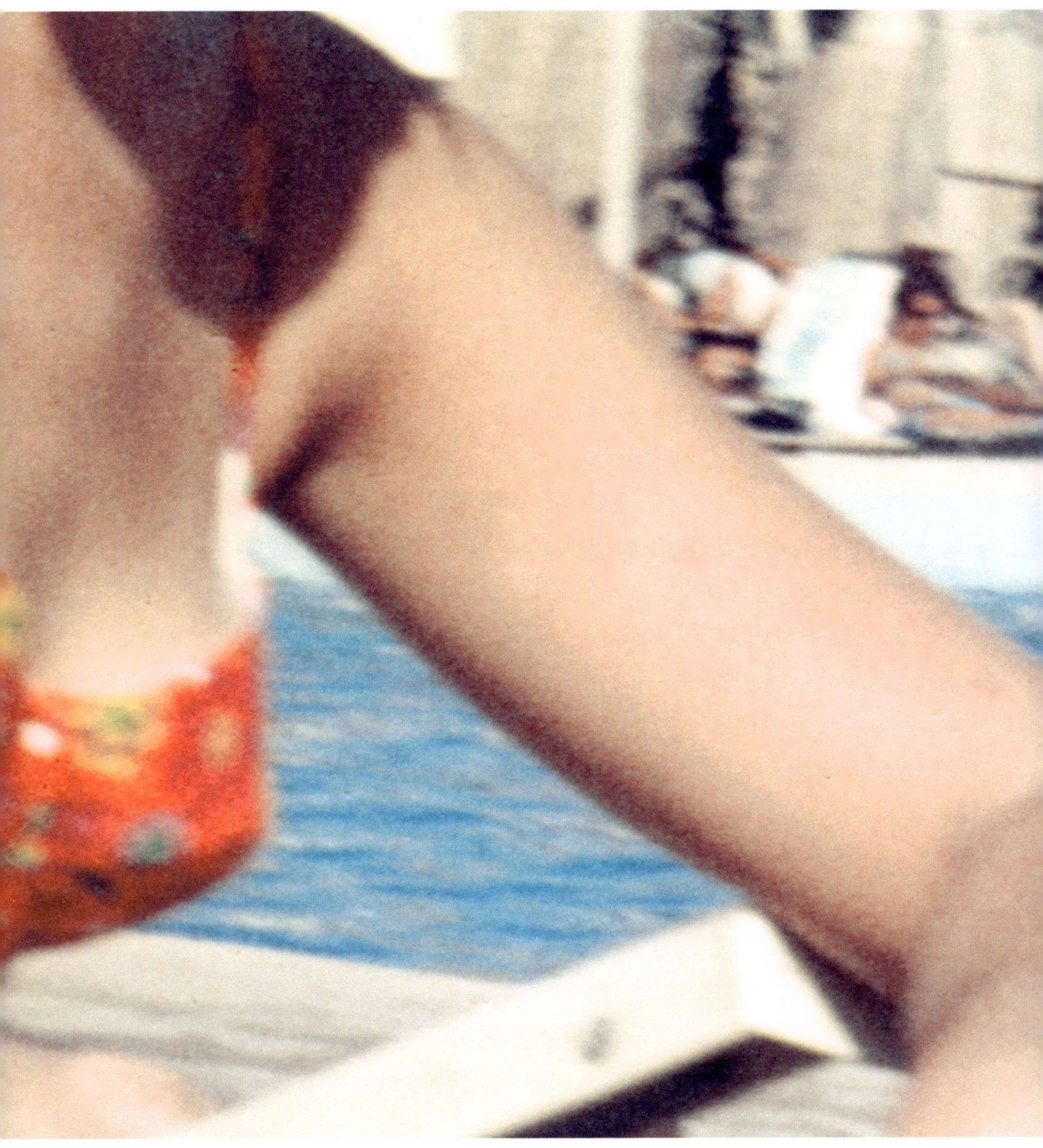

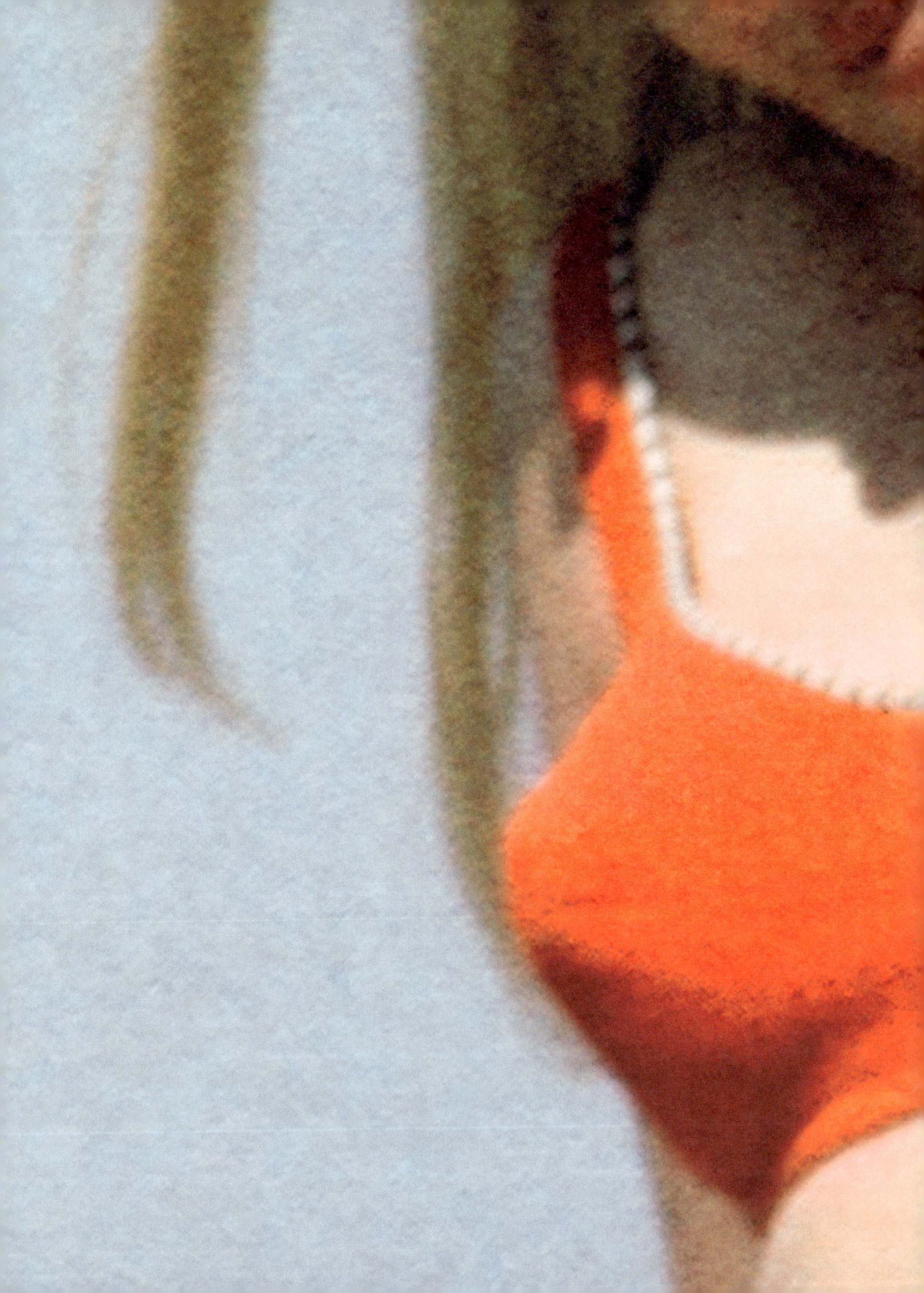

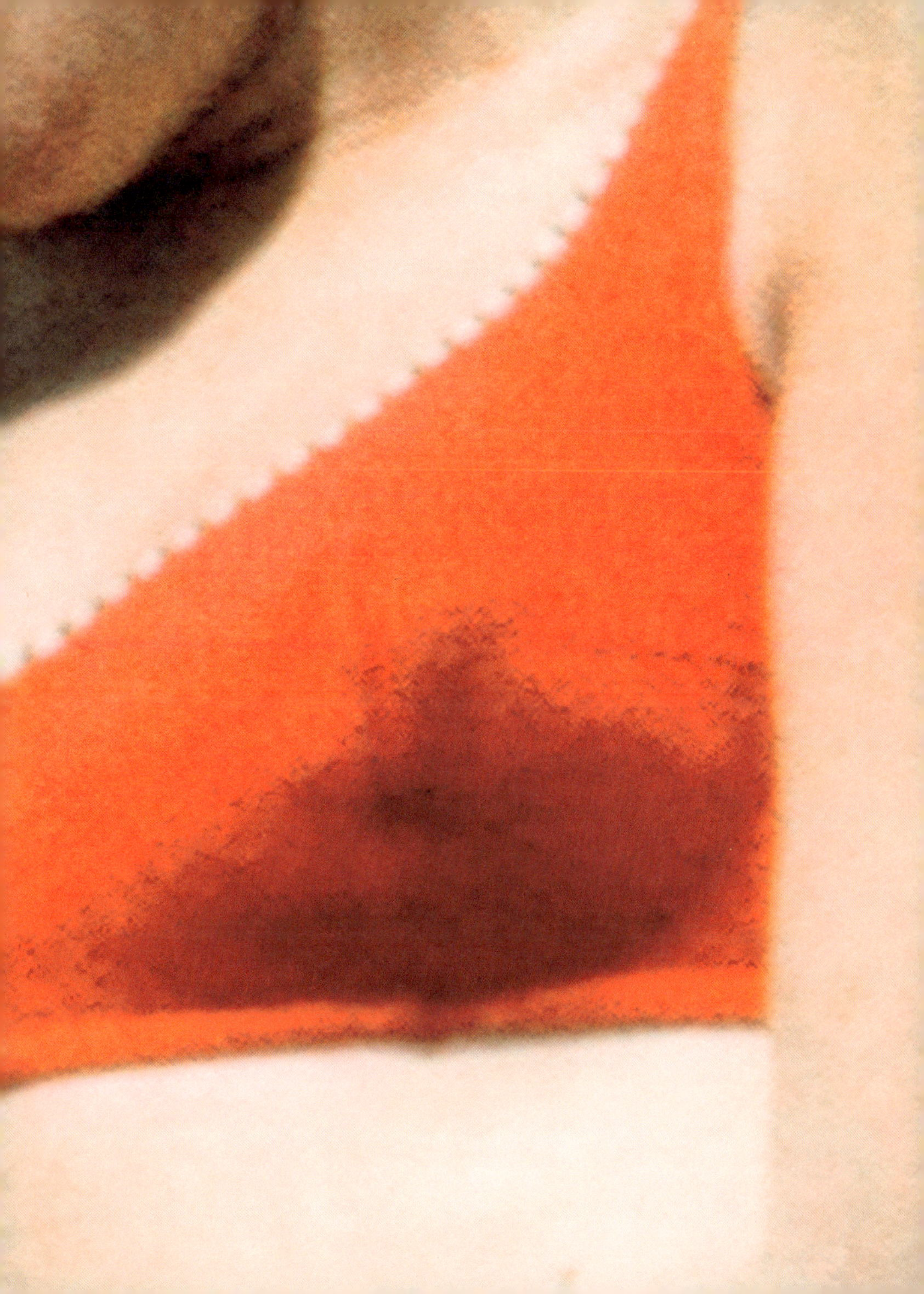

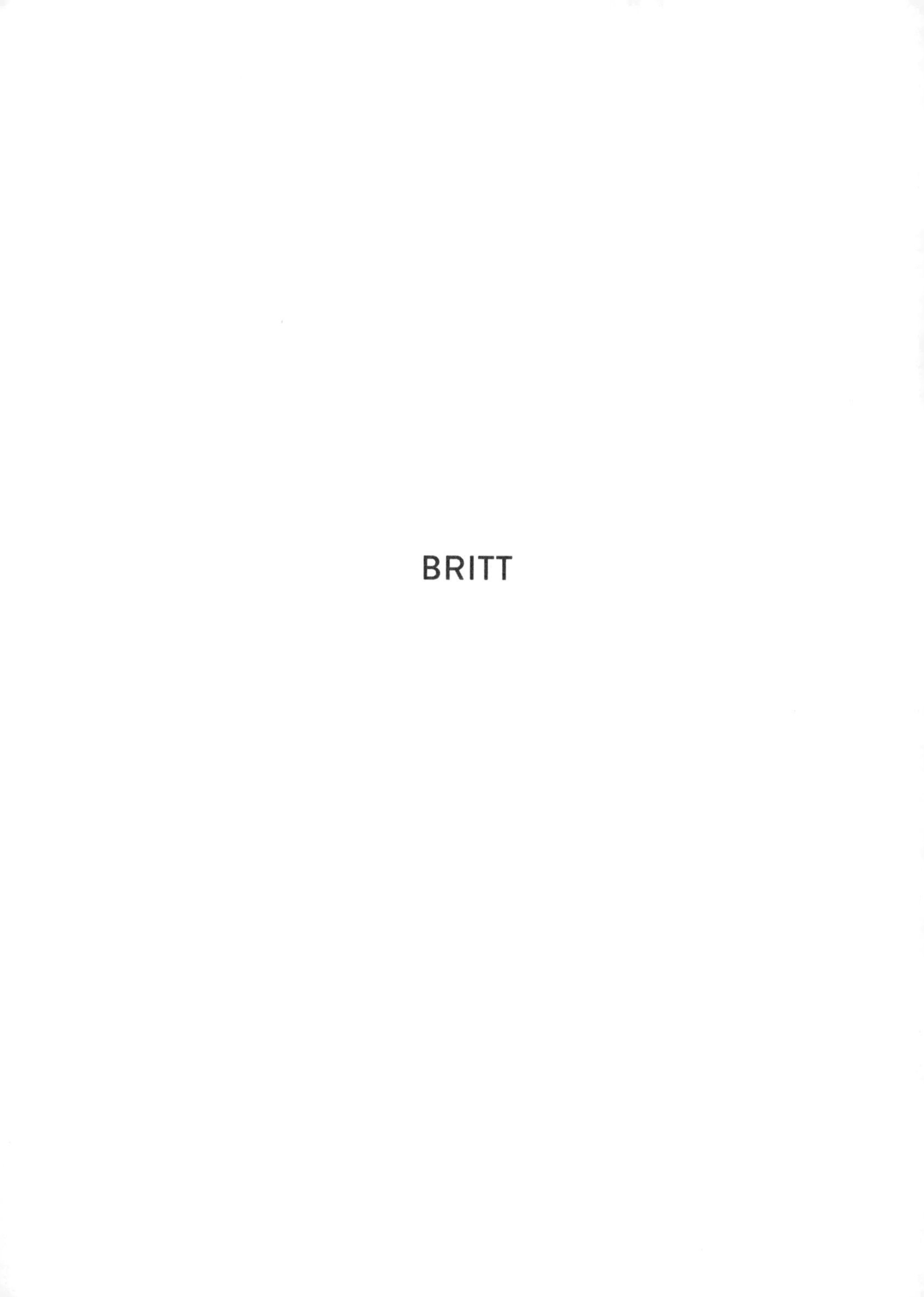

BRITT

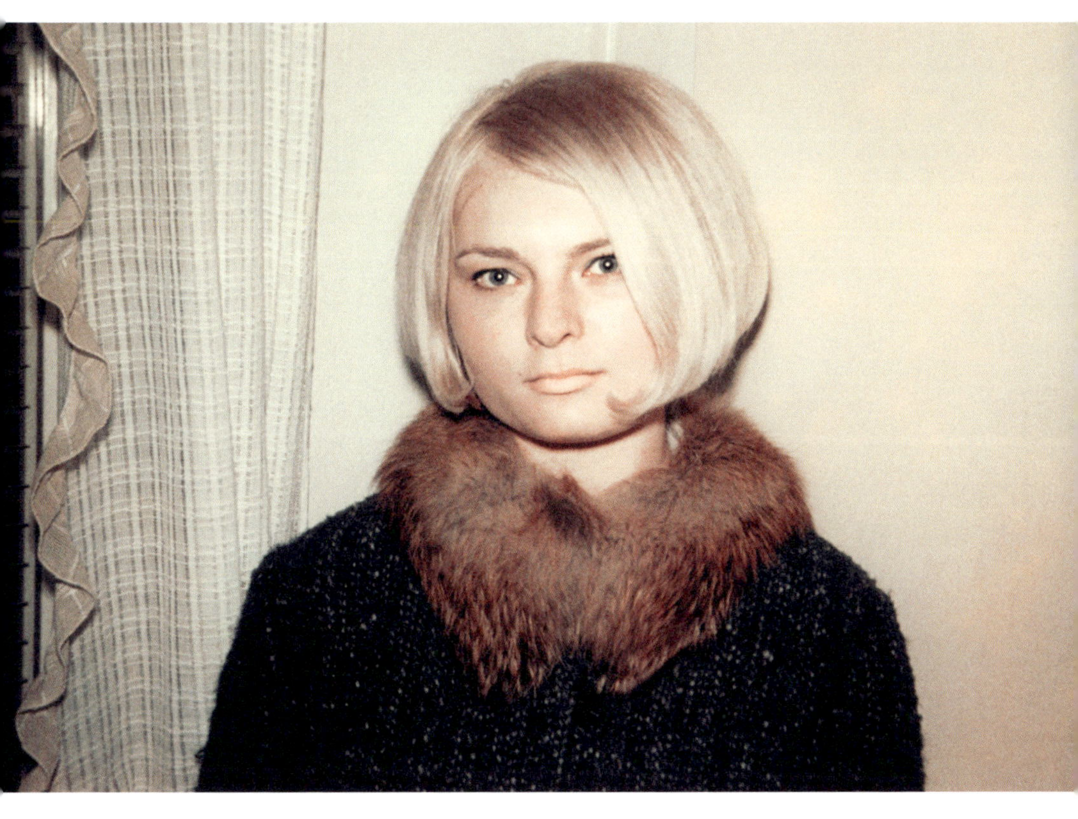

My aunt had a similar coat
from Ohlssons in Malmö.

The frill on the curtain reminds me
of my grandparents' flat in Ängelholm.

It had a particular smell,
which always made me hold my nose.

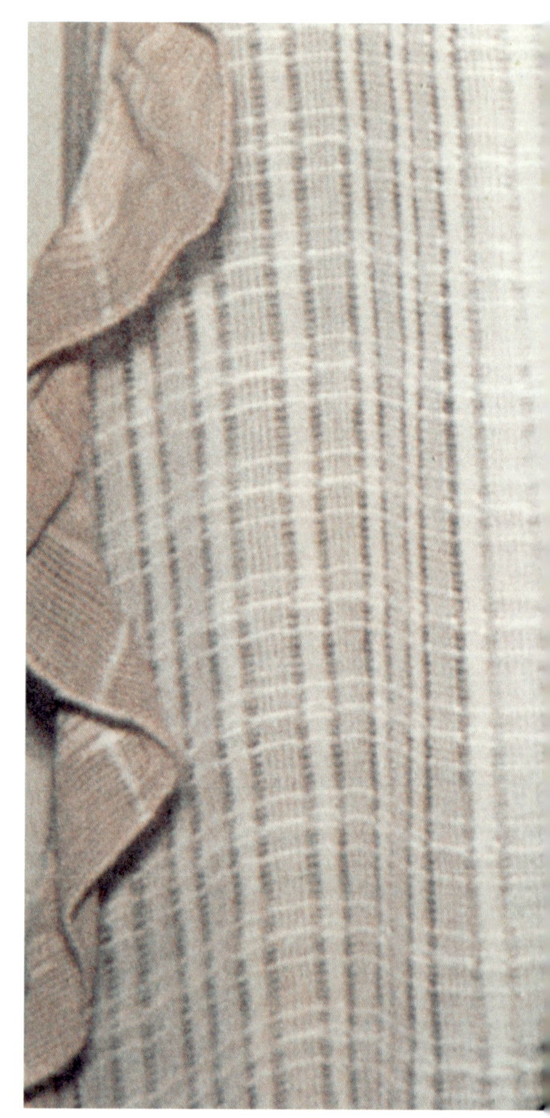

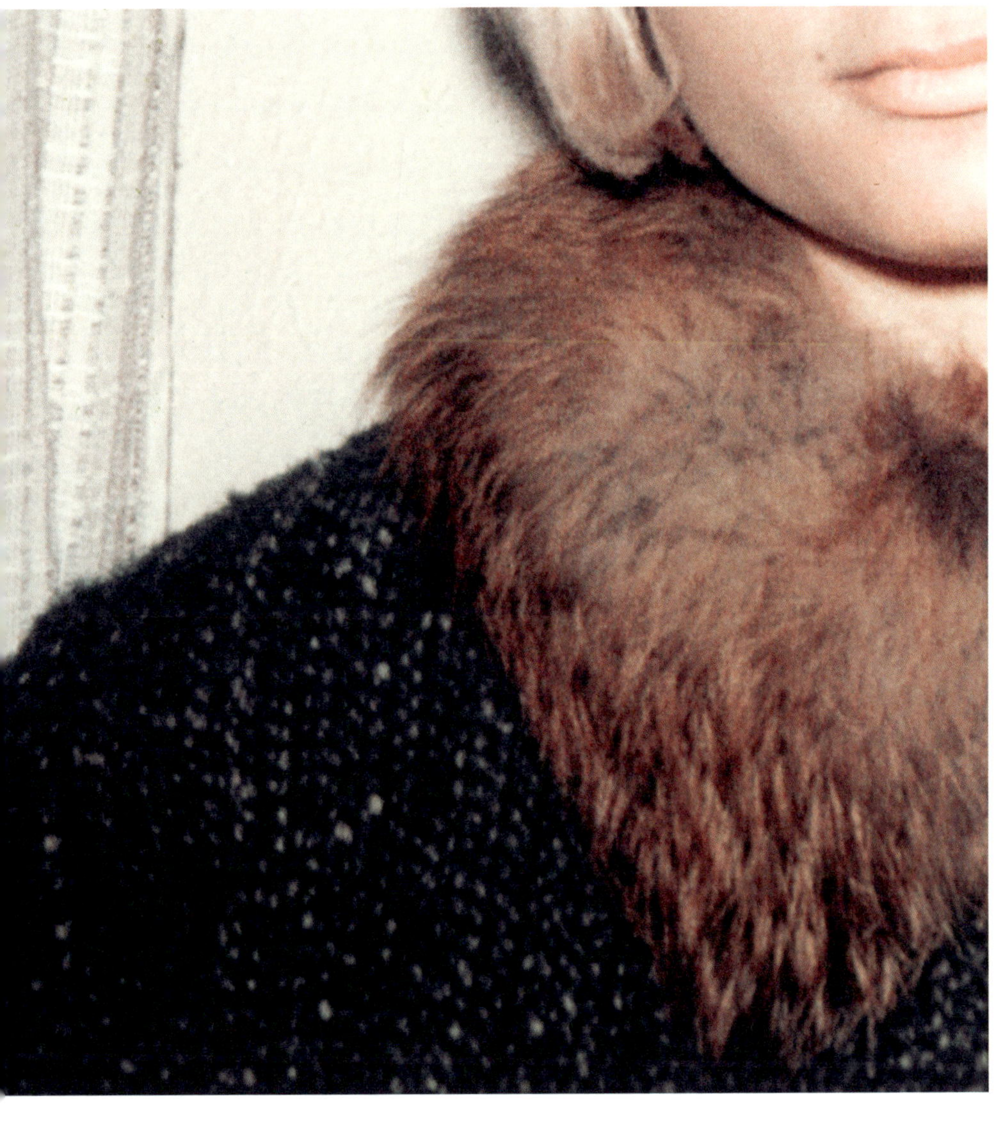

The slides were stored in a
cardboard box in the spare room
(along with the rest of life's remnants).

I expected Nigerian moths and butterflies
(collected during National Service),
or possibly pea growing in southern Sweden
(when he worked for Findus).

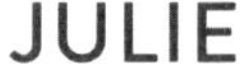
JULIE

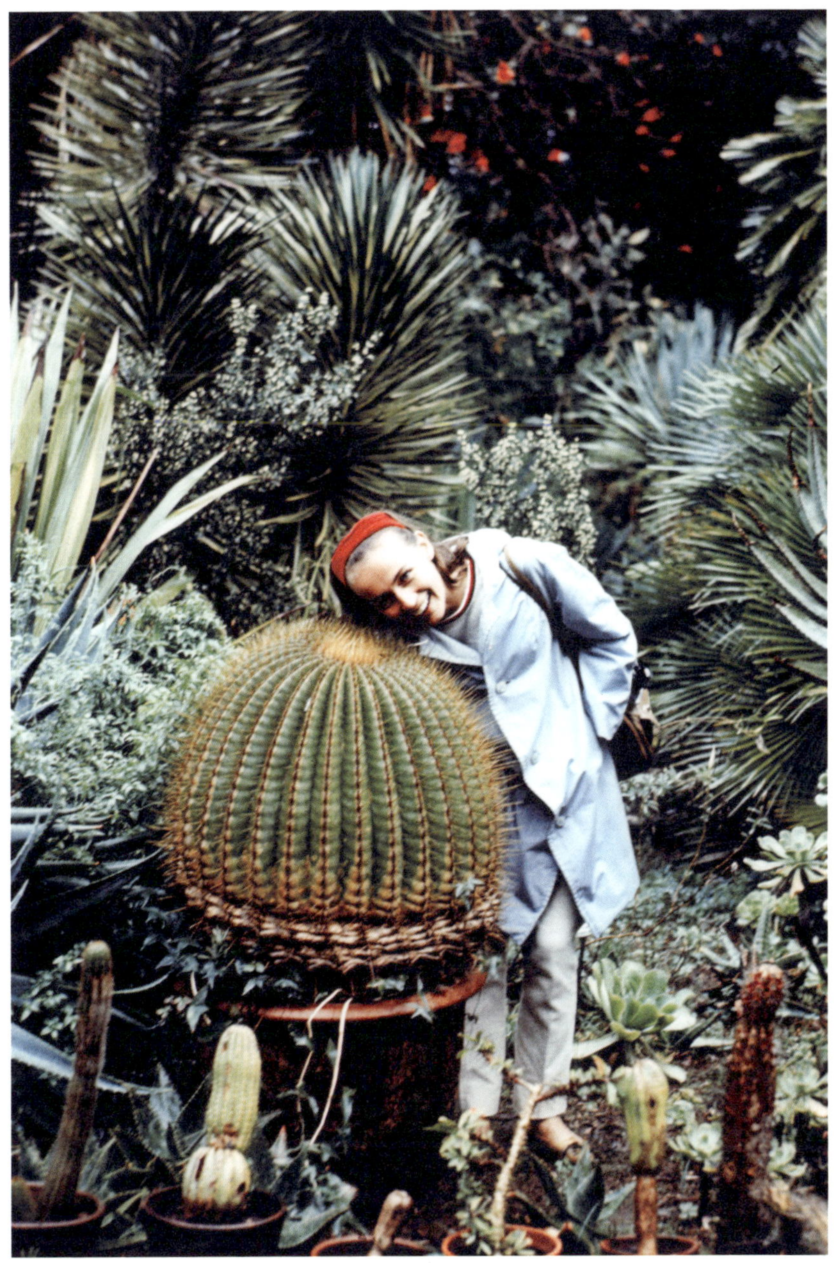

The first slide I picked.

I put it into the Solar Colour viewer,
and saw this beautiful smile beaming
up at me through time.

Strange how she can be looking
at me and looking at him.

It was exhilarating.

It took a while before I noticed
the row of smaller cacti standing
firmly to attention along the bottom
of the frame.

My parents used to have a black and
white print of the Kama Sutra on the
wall above their bed.

When I got older it was replaced
by a watercolour of a country house.

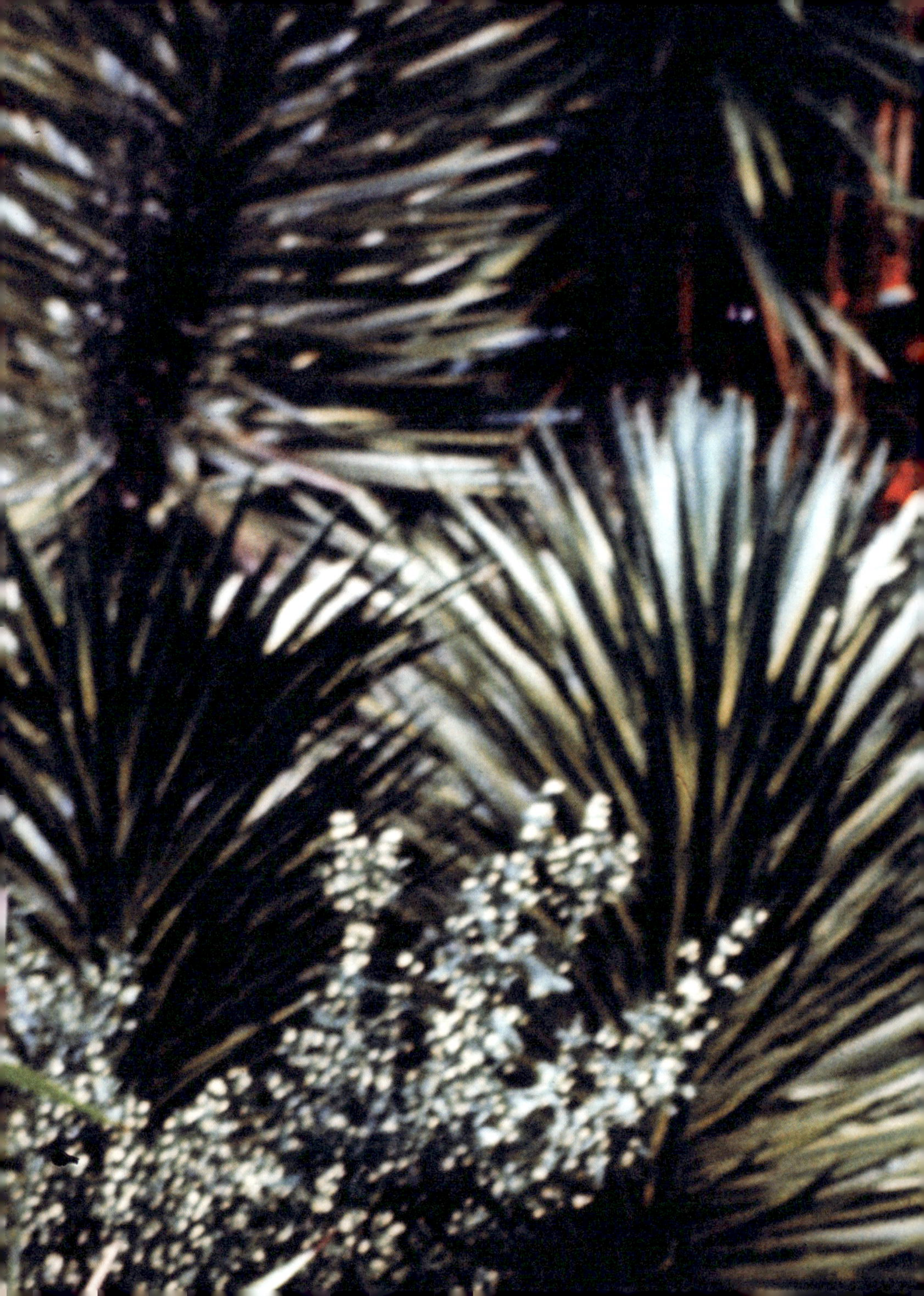

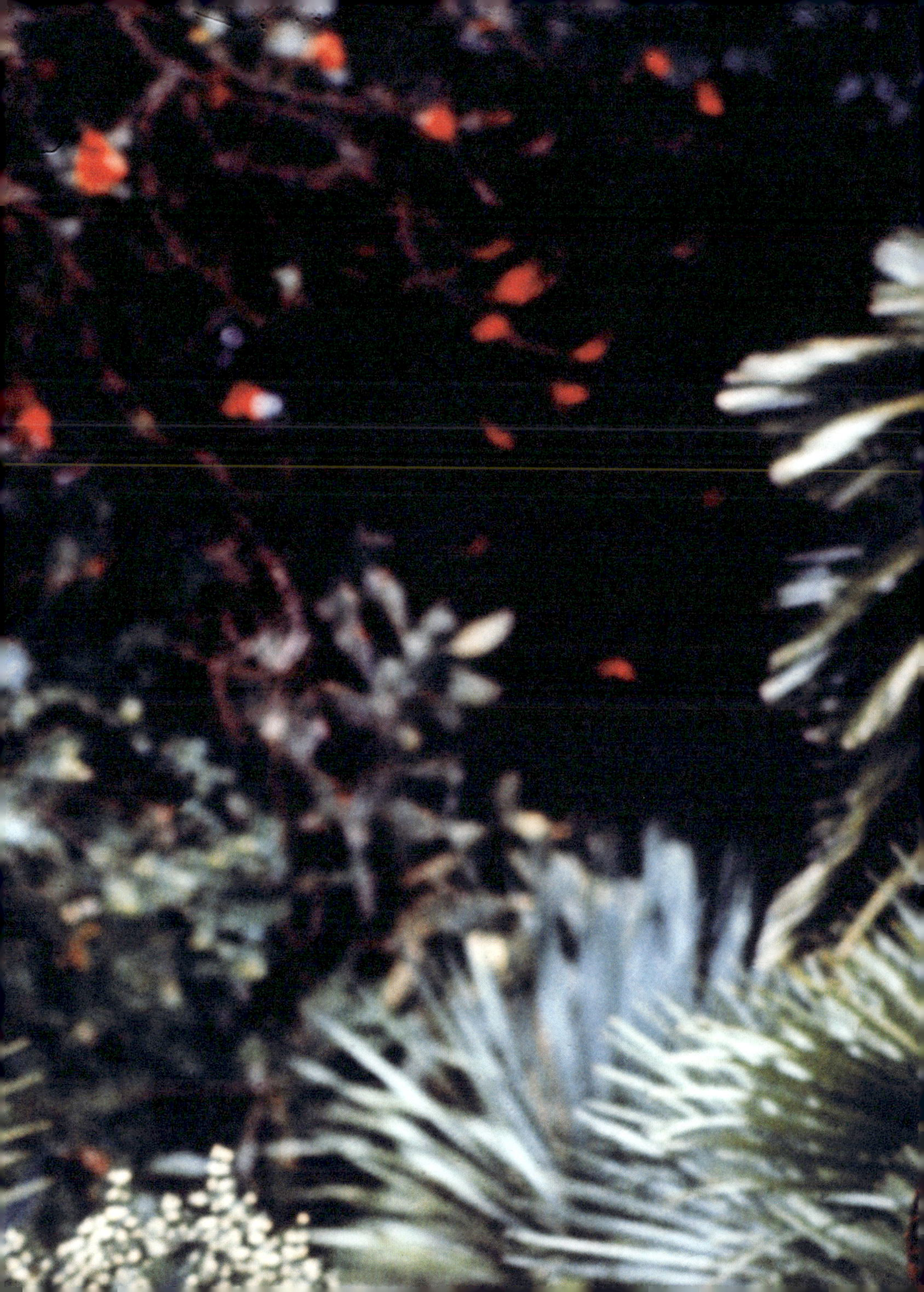

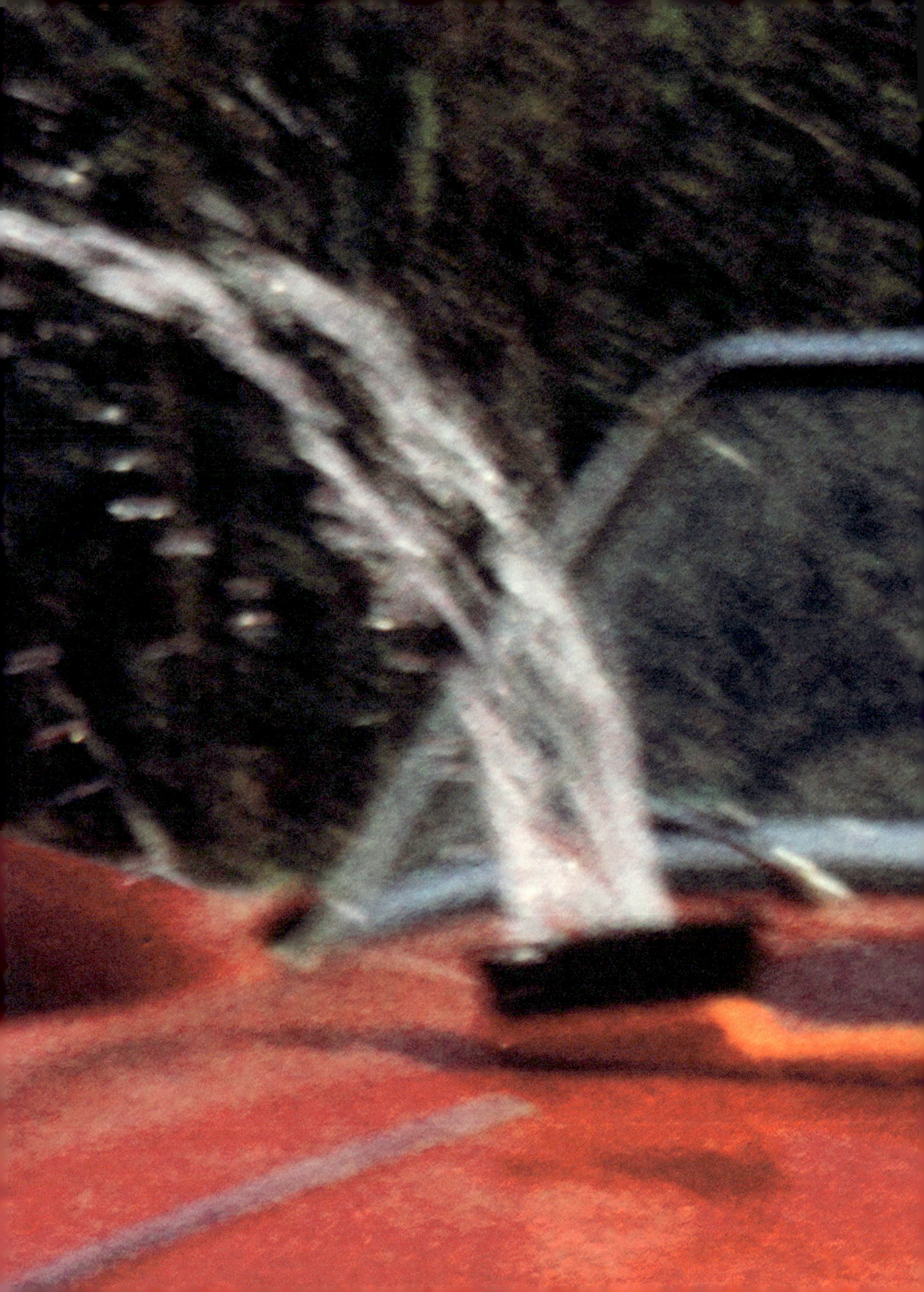

Her white sports car (gleaming)
is parked next to his red sports car (filthy).

She has finished washing hers, and it looks
as if she is about to start washing his.

(He would give me 50p for it.)

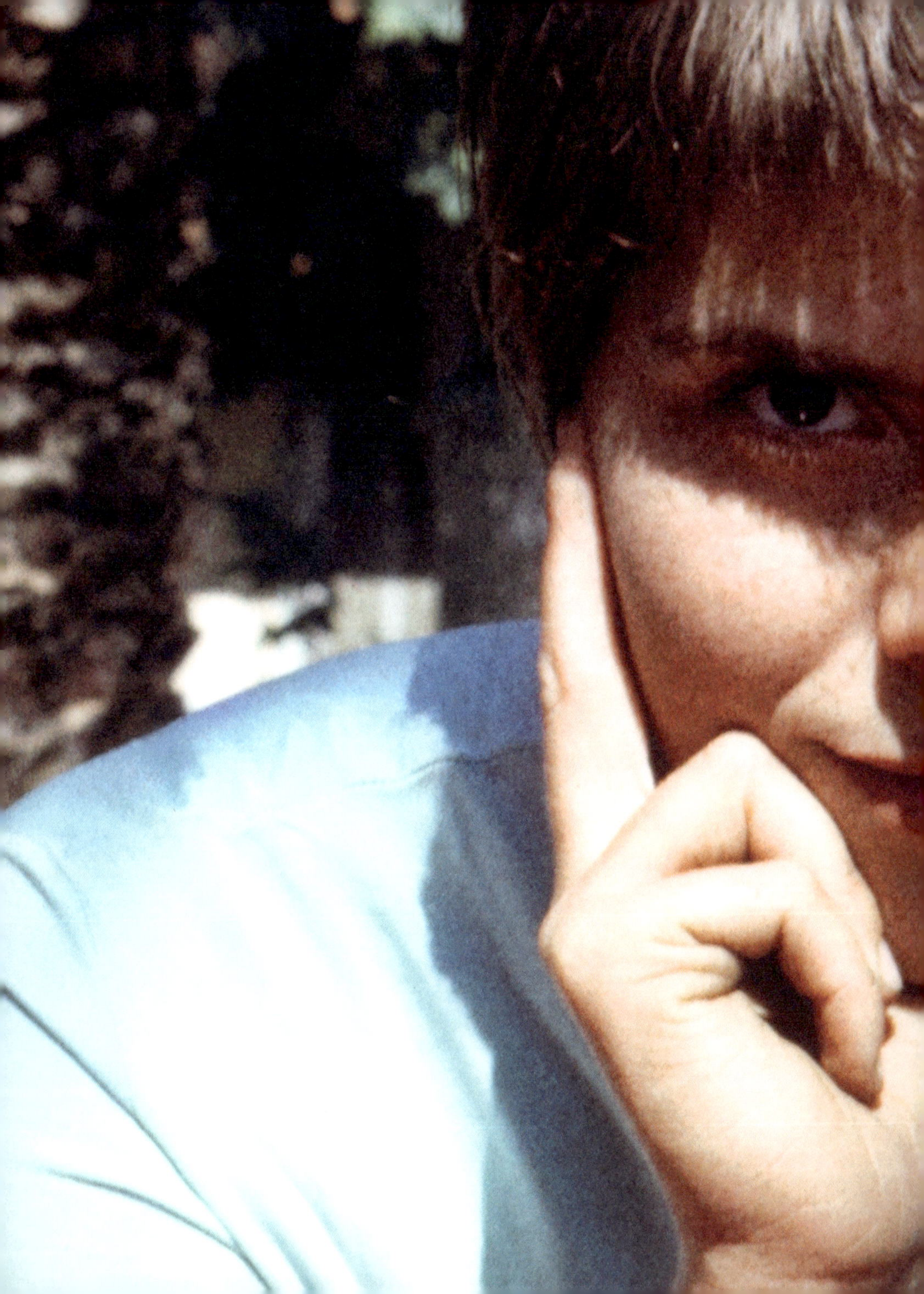

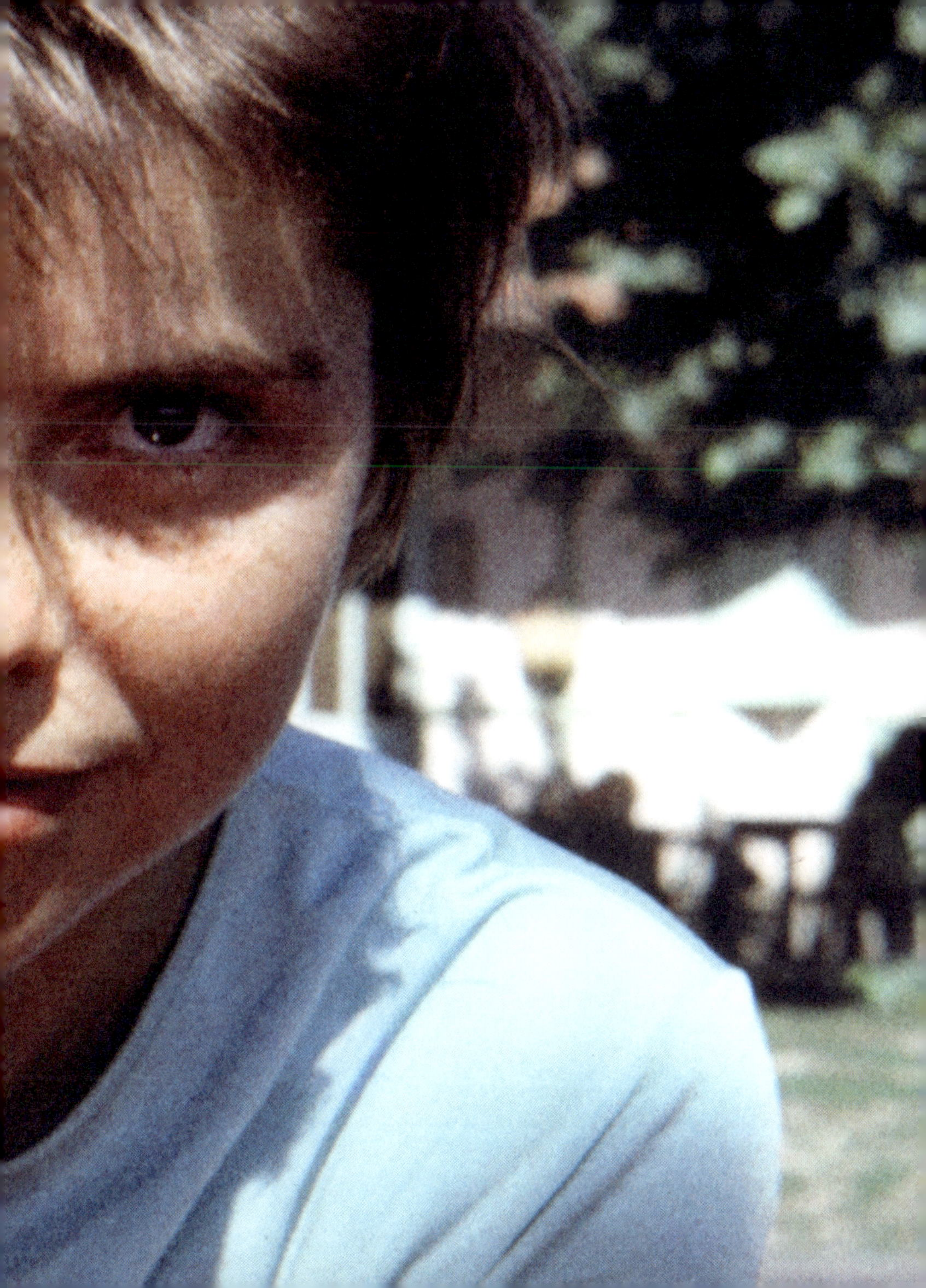

For my eleventh birthday
my dad gave me a Konica Tomato.
I took photographs of flowers
and made them into cards.
(He hoped I would be an entrepreneur.)

I loved to watch his cine films
(curtains drawn, screen rolled down,
projector threaded and whirring).

The one I remember most vividly
is a close up of a red squirrel nibbling
a pine cone outside my grandparents'
summer house.

I could smell the poplars.

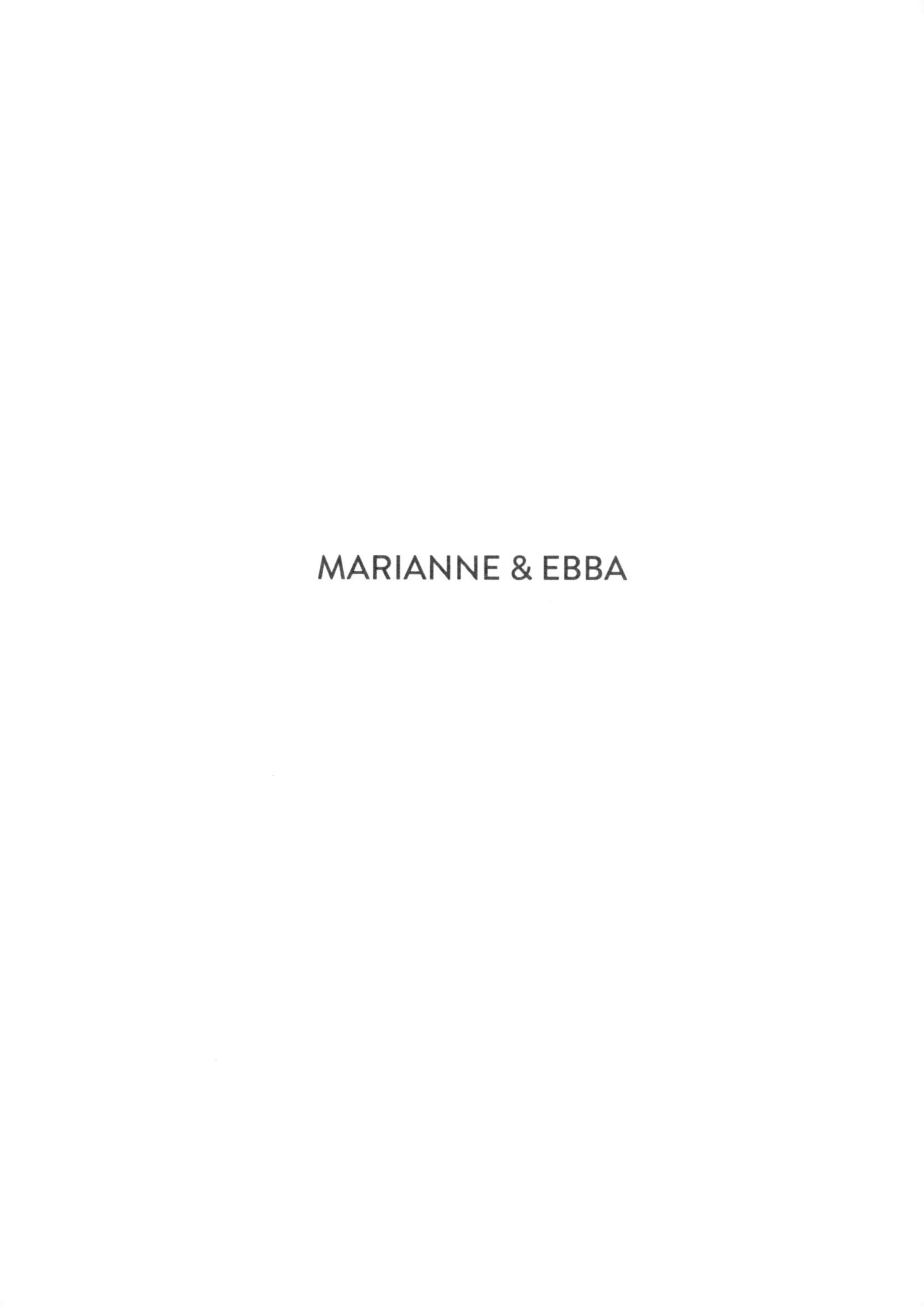

MARIANNE & EBBA

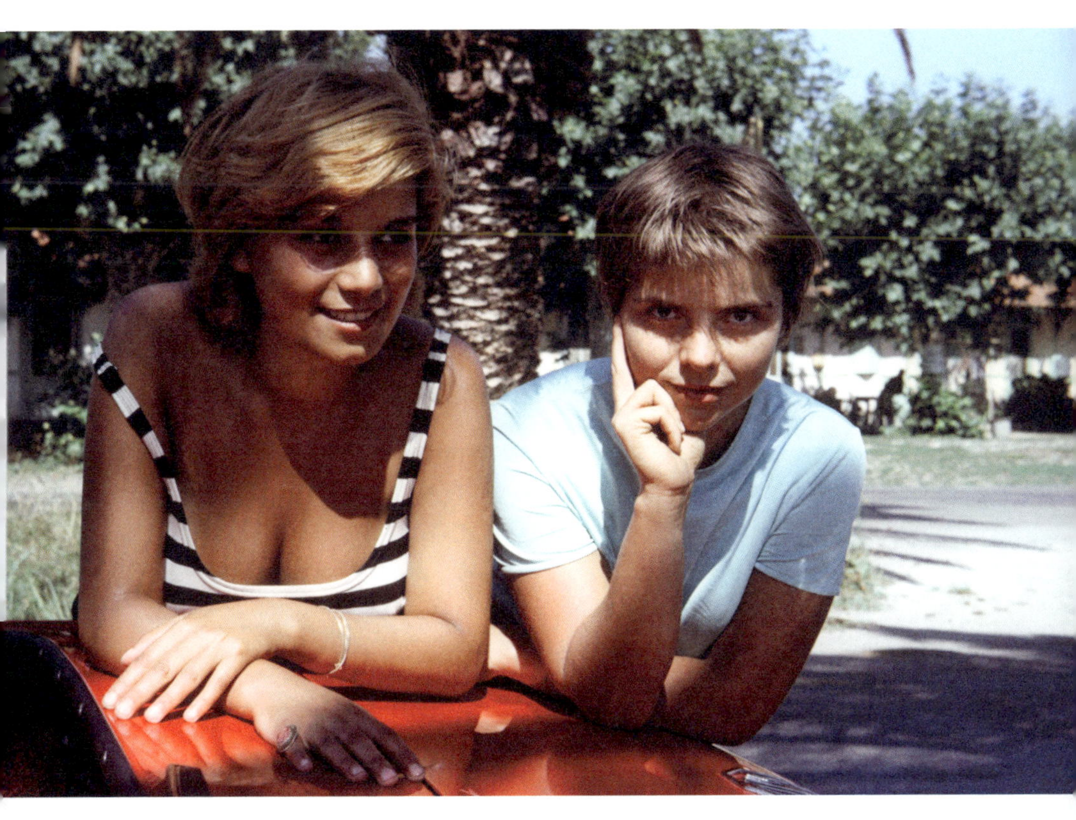

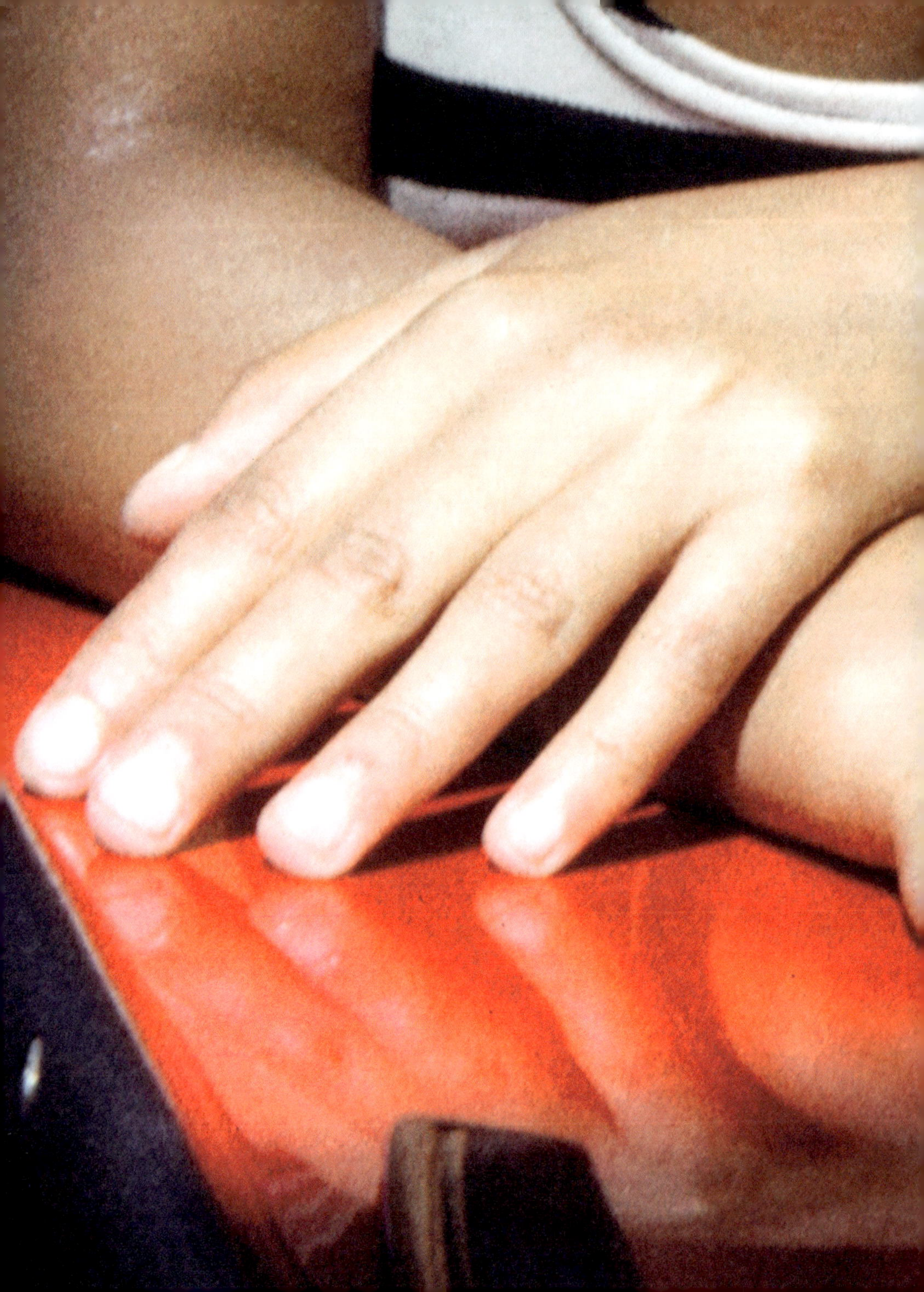

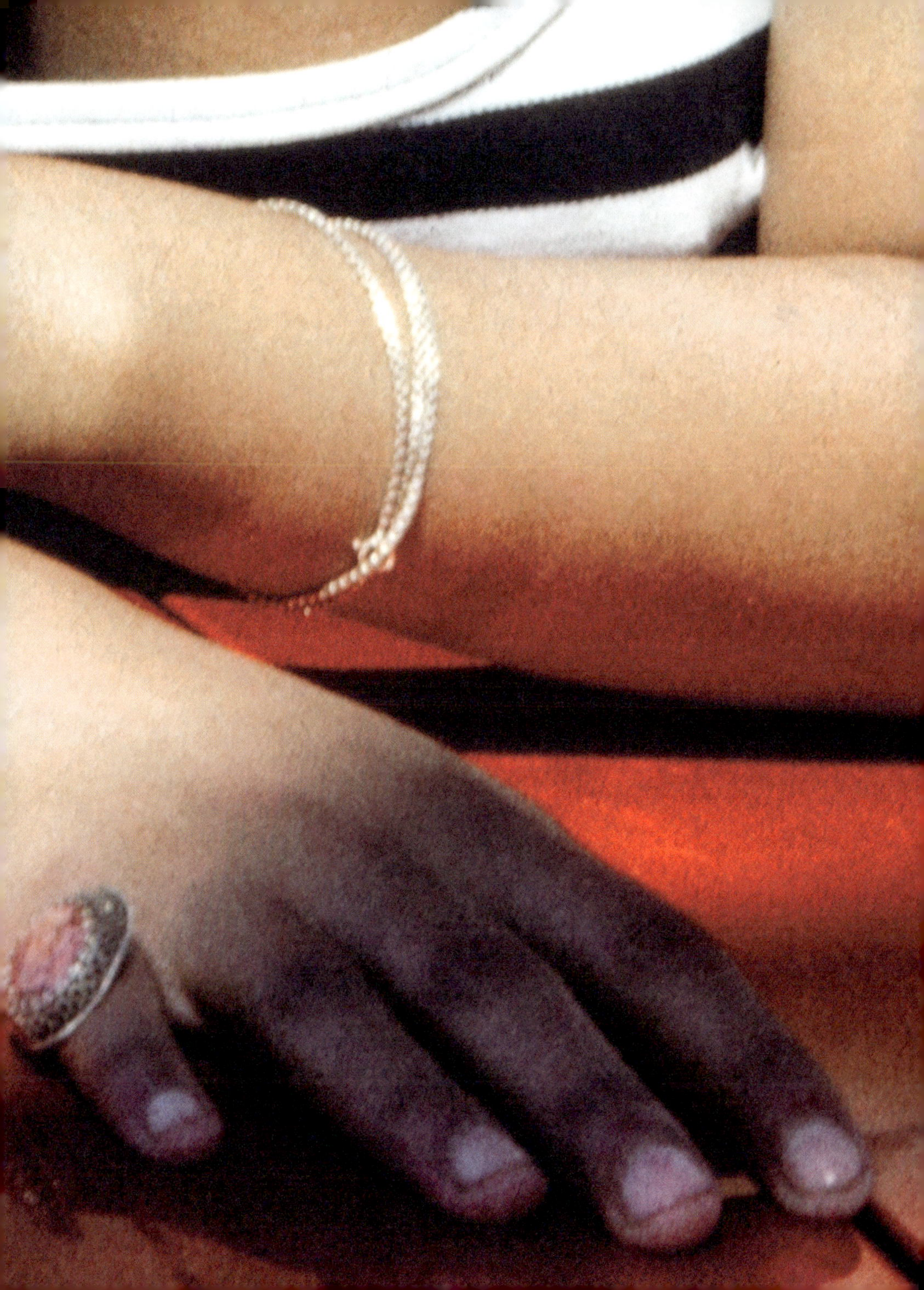

He took a road trip with
friends to the South of France.

There's a photo of Marianne standing on
the car boot, looking like Marilyn Monroe.
He's standing next to her,
arm around her waist.

He's wearing blue swimming shorts
and his feet are bare.

He looks carefree.

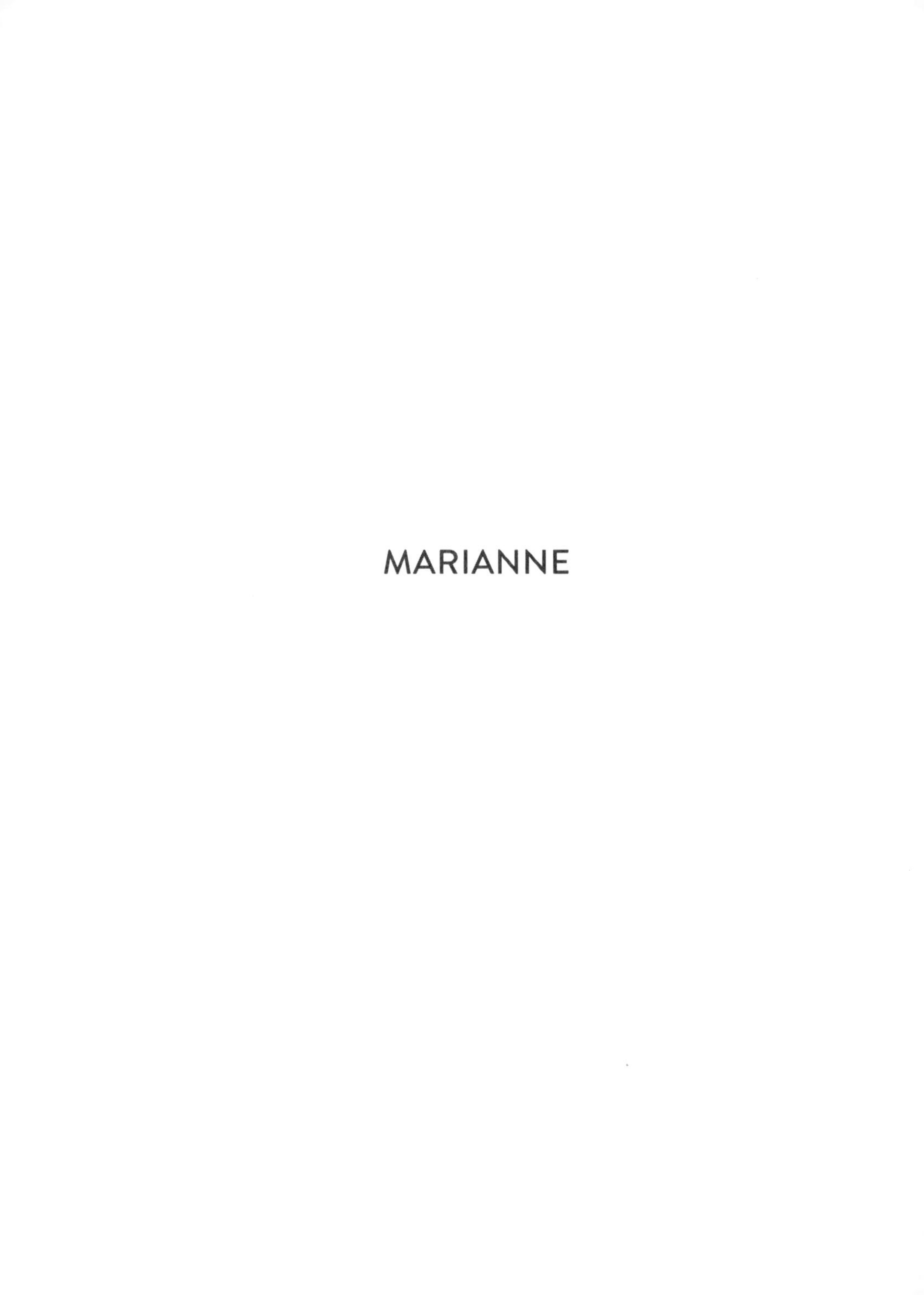

MARIANNE

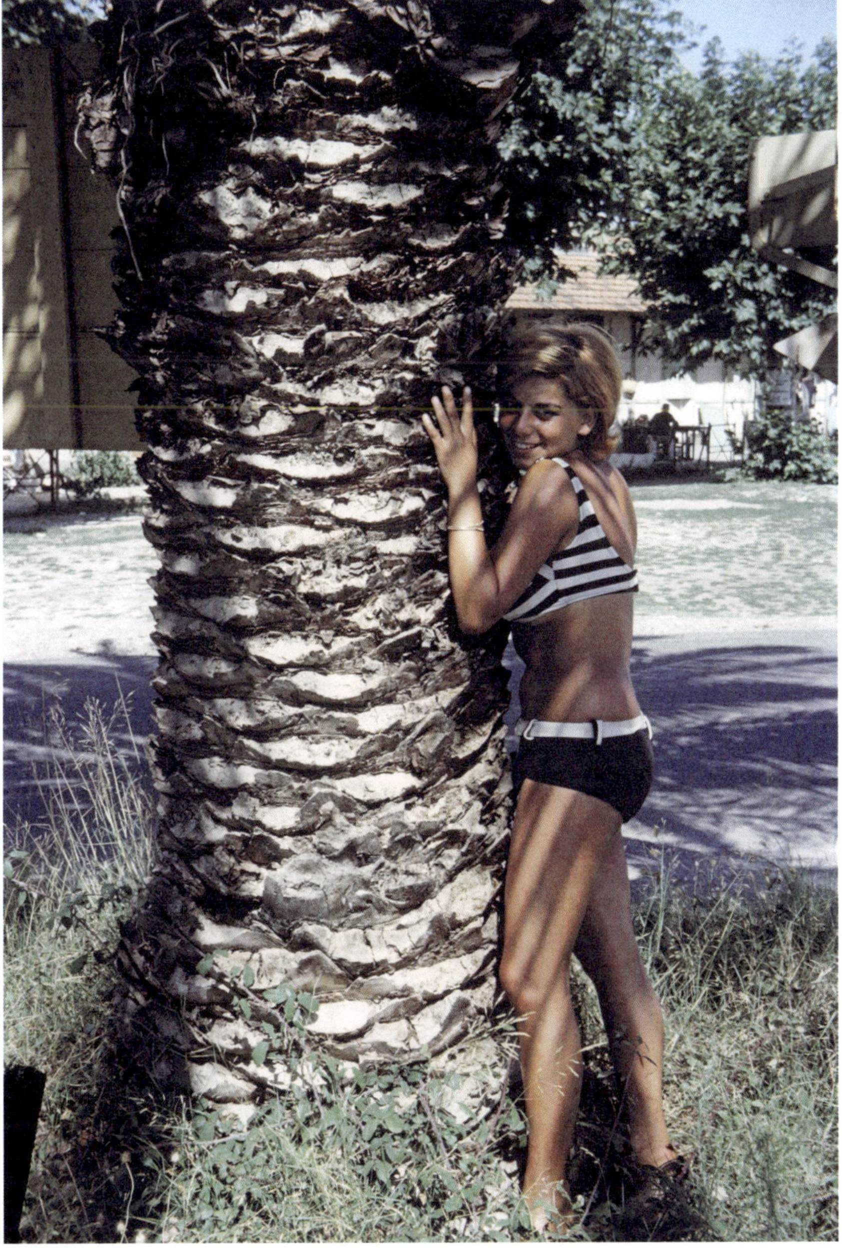

When I got my first job
he came to meet me for lunch.

He had his usual sandwich in his briefcase.
Two squares (lunch slowed him down, he said).
But I suggested we buy some from the café.
He thought they were delicious.

It was the first time I remember seeing him
out of context.

He looked smaller somehow.

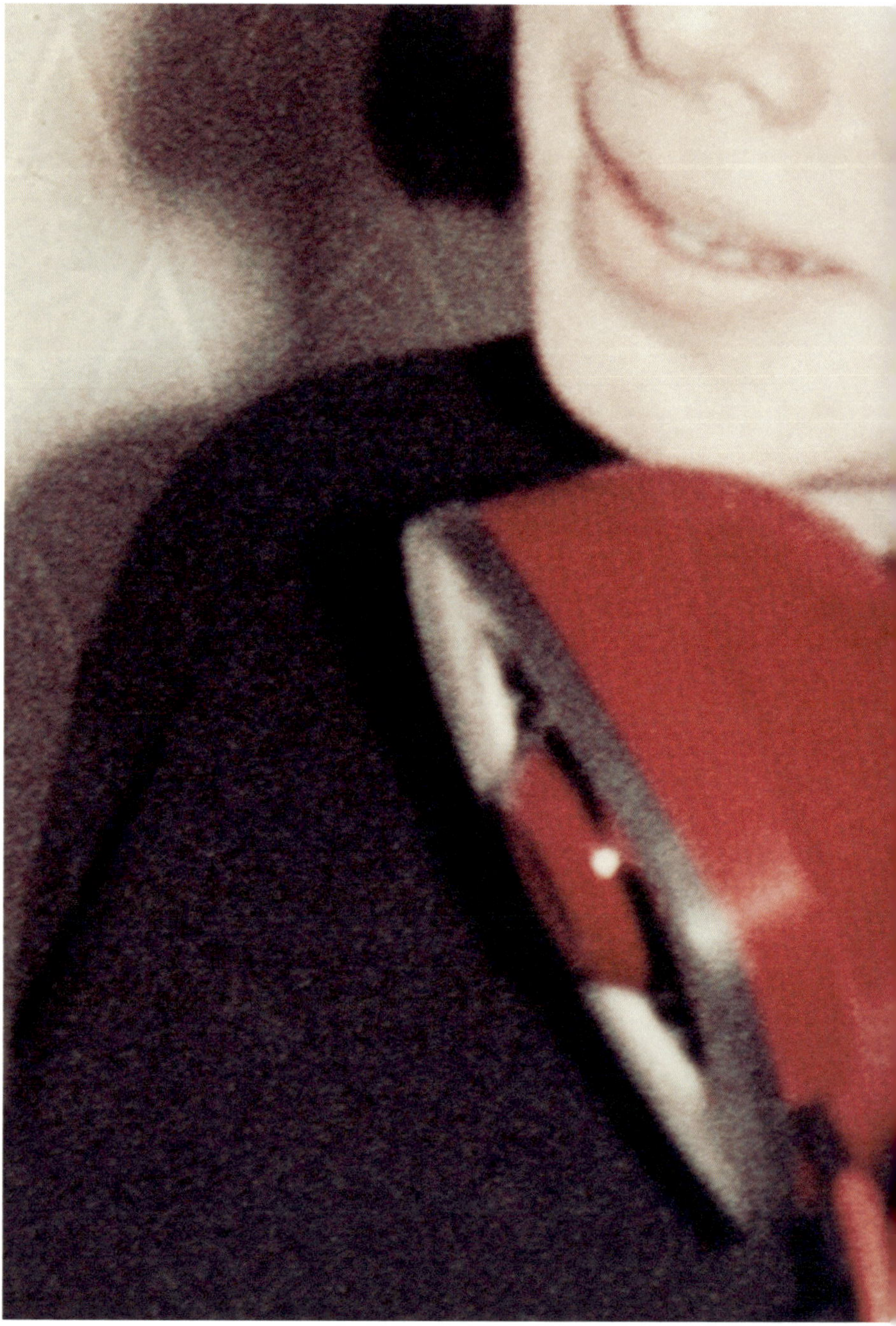

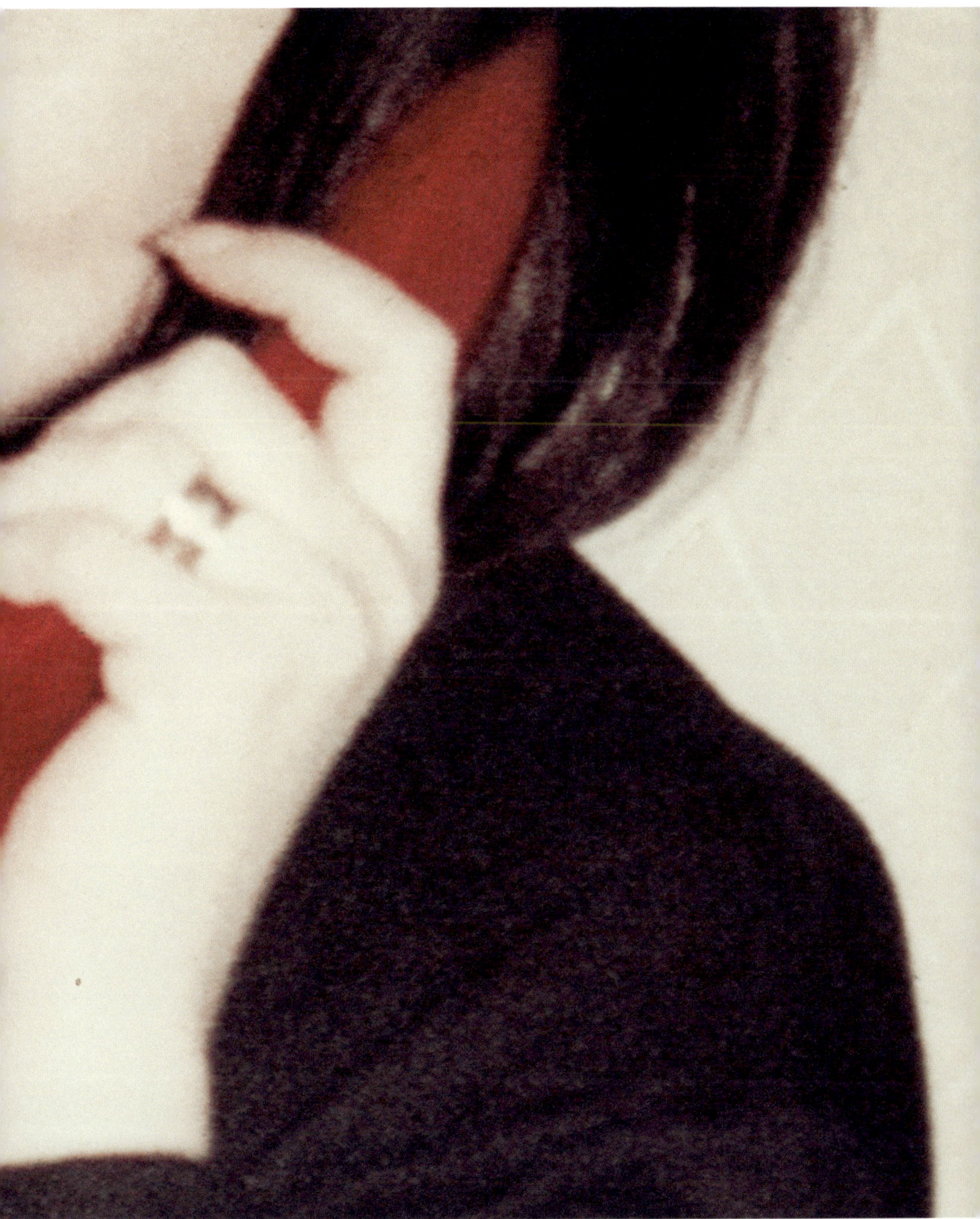

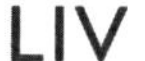
LIV

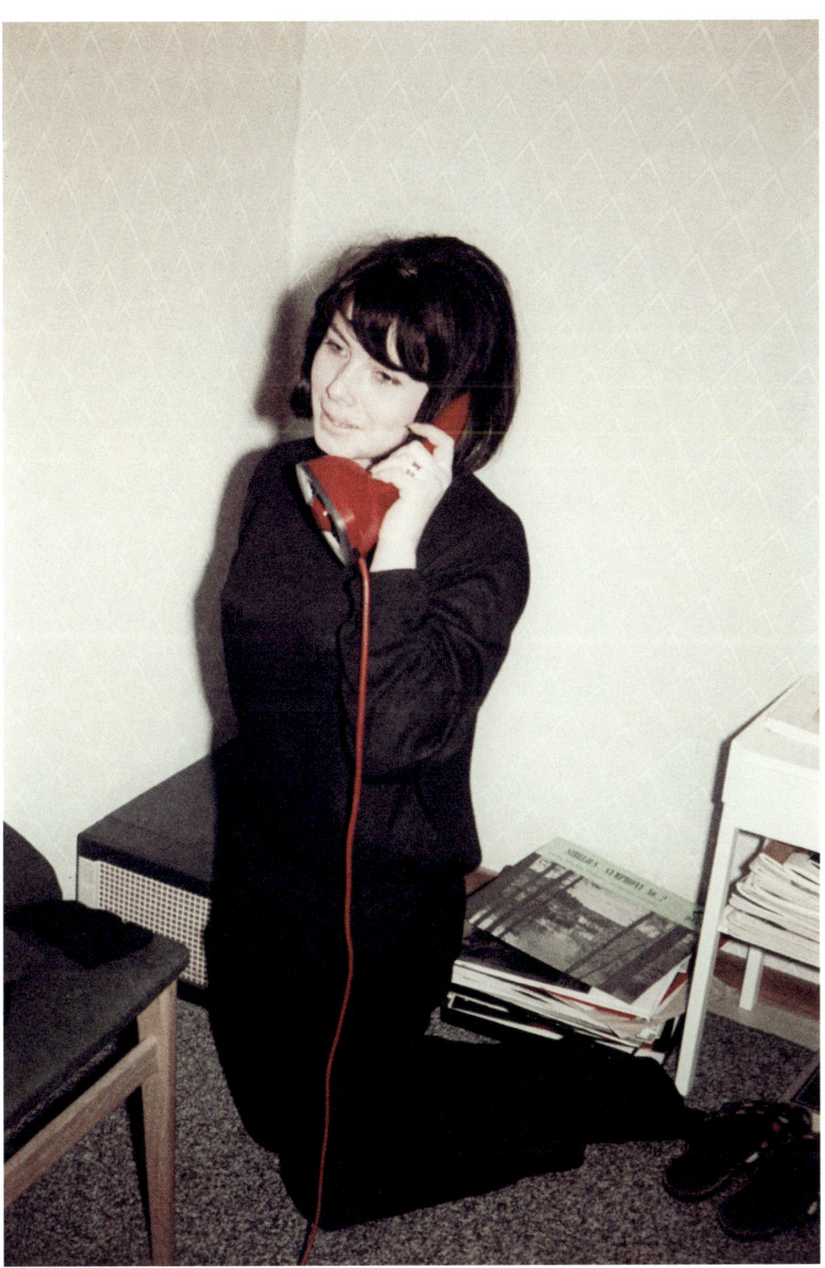

It must be the inside of his flat,
near Helsingborg.

He moved there after university
(to get away from his stepmother
and explore his Motherland).

He liked to listen to Sibelius' Symphony No. 2,
alone, when we disappeared to Sweden
for the long summer holidays.

(My mother prefers Rod Stewart,
but after he was gone,
she listened to this record every day
for a month.)

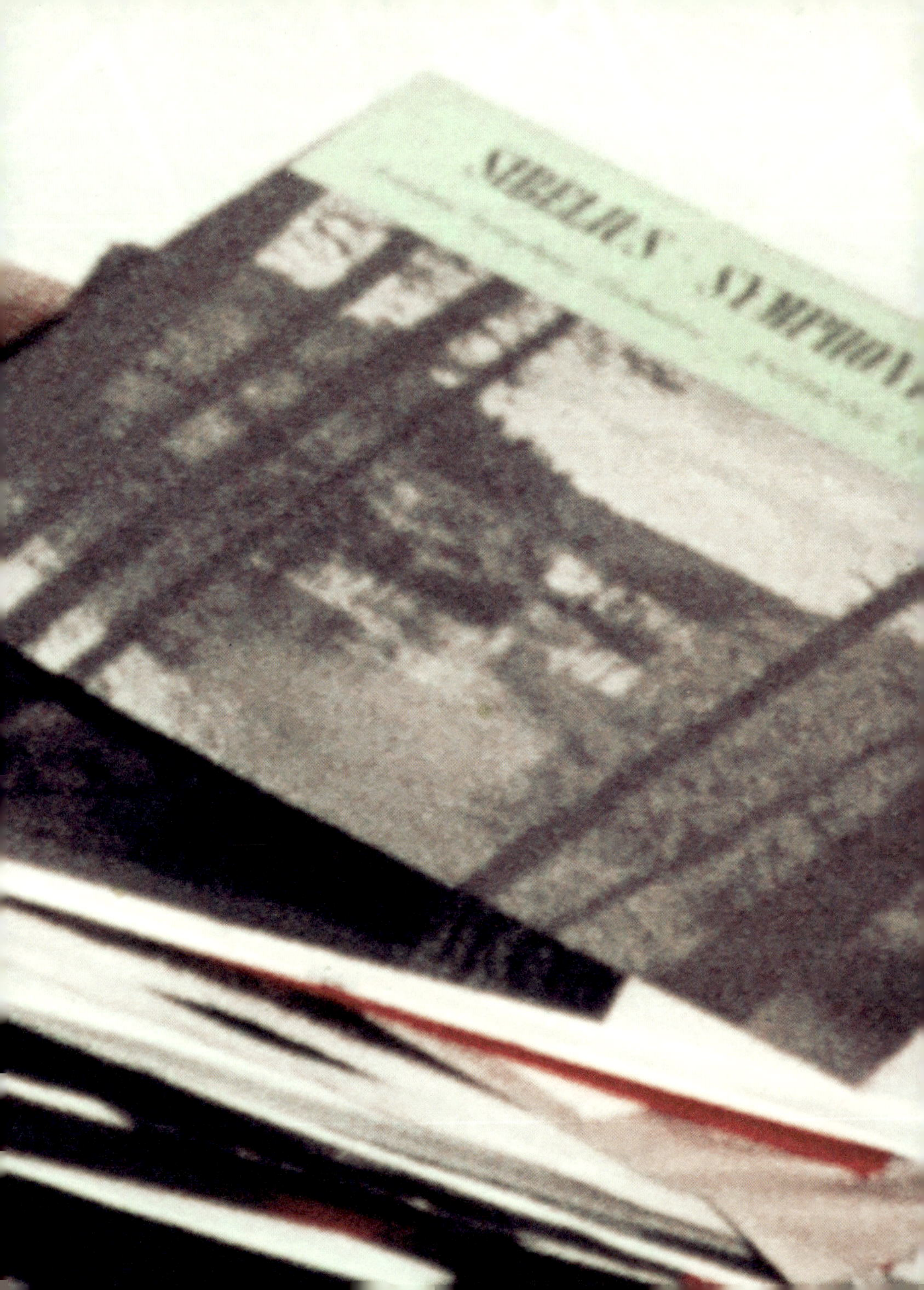
SIBELIUS

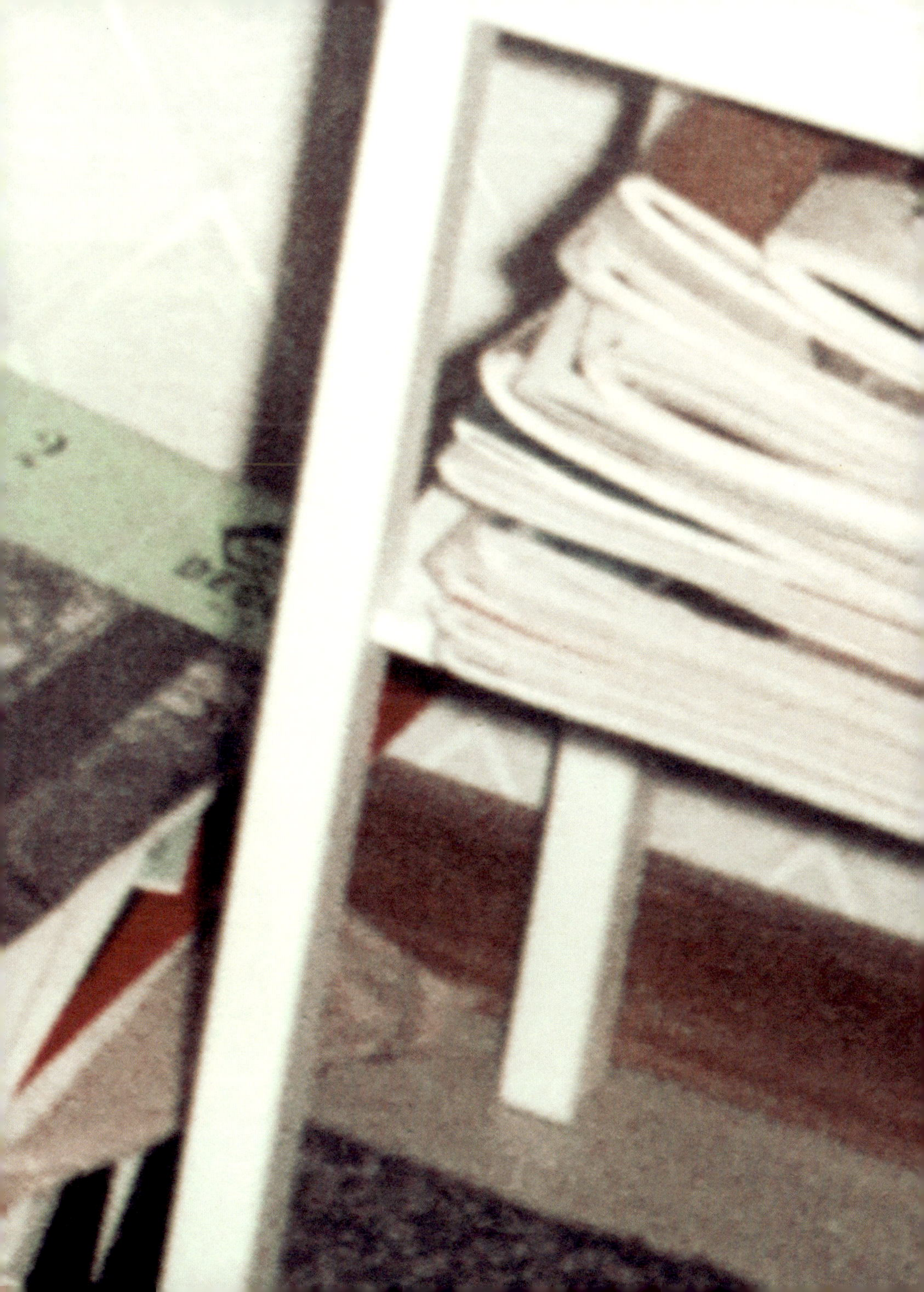

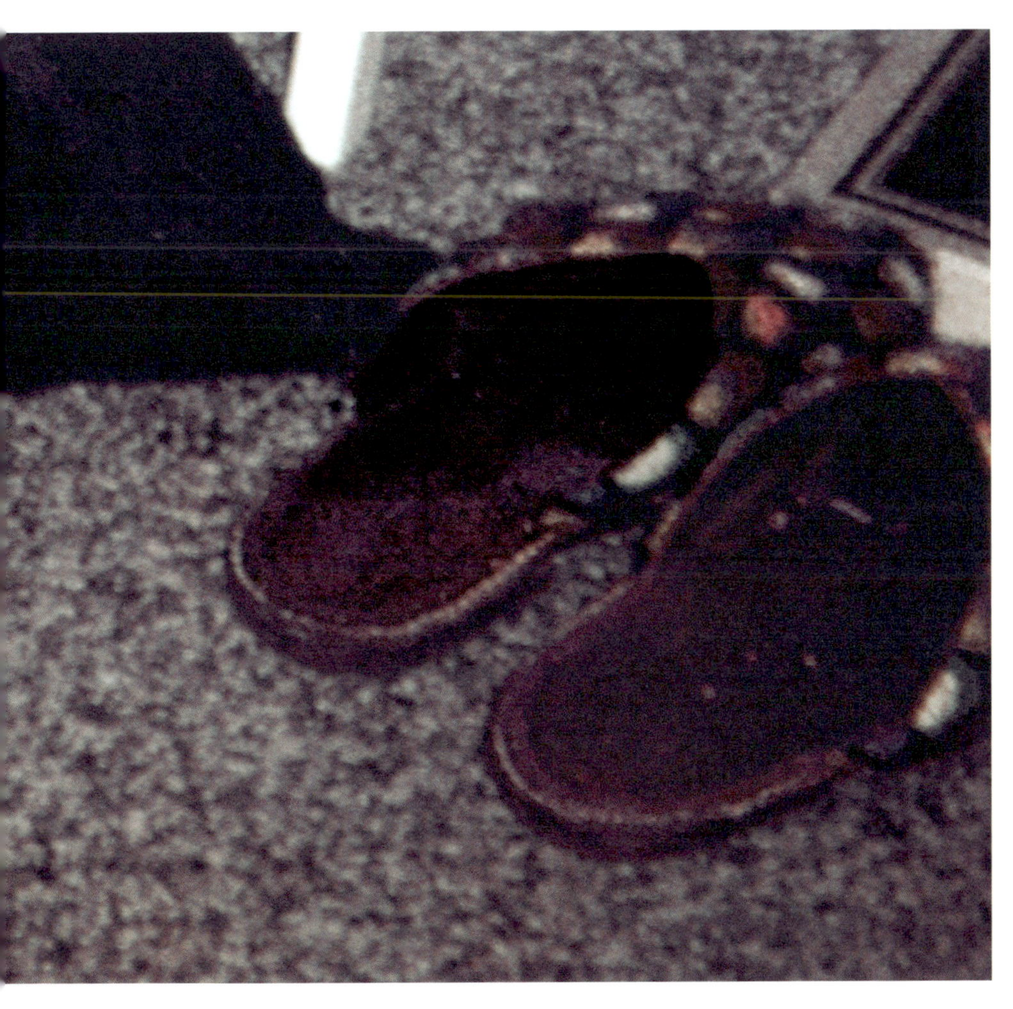

A young version of my father is sitting on the
bonnet of a racing green sports car.
He is looking away from the camera,
gazing out towards the horizon.

He is wearing a white shirt (sleeves rolled up)
and a tie. I imagine that he's come straight from
work. It is a beautiful day and I suspect there is a
beach somewhere nearby.

Caught (accidentally?) in the corner of the frame is
the photographer's shadow. I can tell she is female
not only by the shape, but by the pose that my
father is striking. It is relaxed yet commanding,
a pose with which he intends to impress.

I scrutinise this young man who is a stranger to me. He looks tall and slim with a fringe of fair hair swept to one side across his forehead. (The style he would maintain for the rest of his life.)

He appears as confident in front of the camera as he is behind it. It is striking that his countenance is so serious (that he is taking himself so seriously).
I recognise the strong jaw line (is it clenched?).

Printed along the right hand side it says *Sep 66*.
He would have been twenty eight, nearly twenty nine, and still living in Sweden.

It is eight years since the death of his mother and three years before he will meet his future wife.

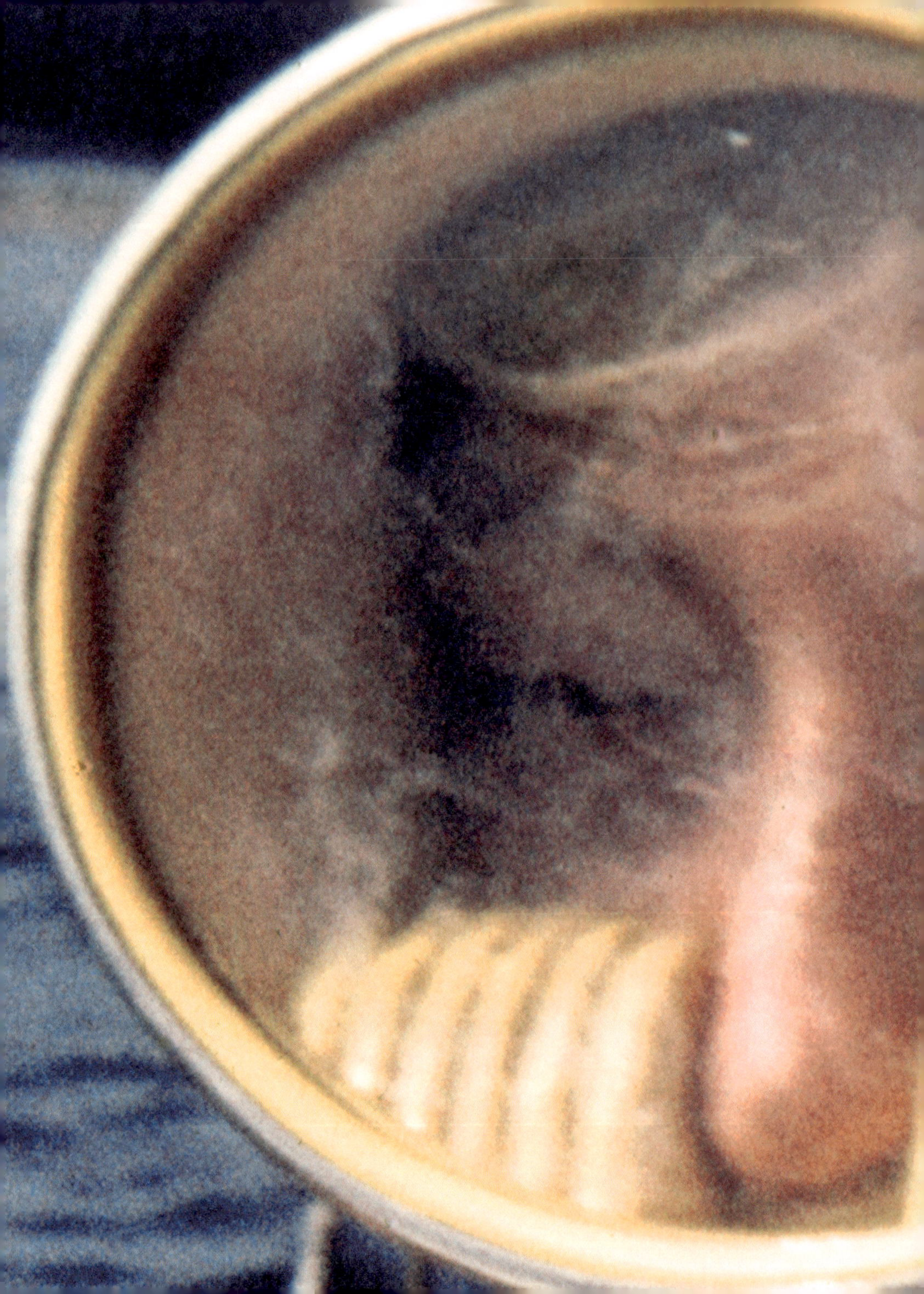

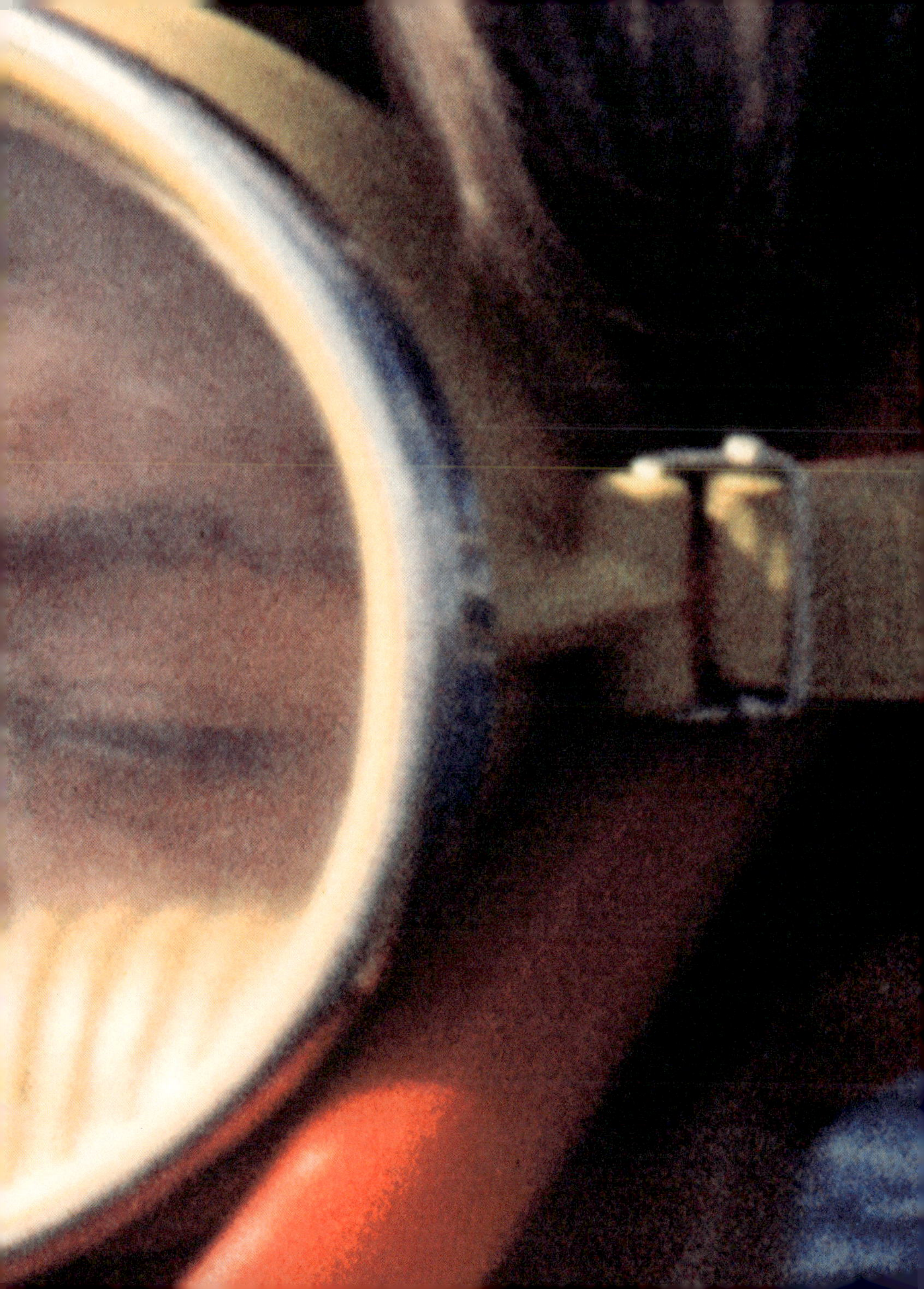

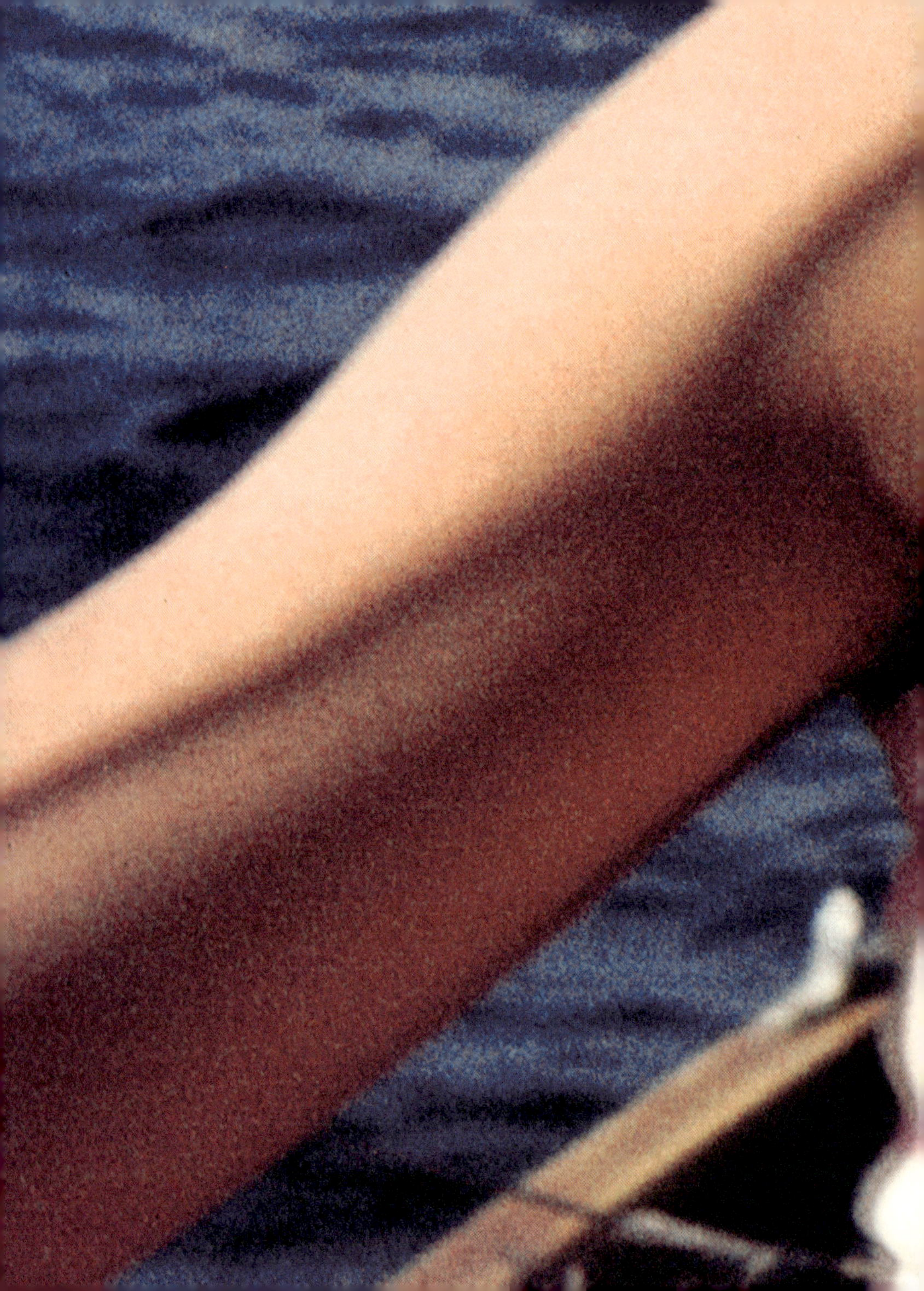

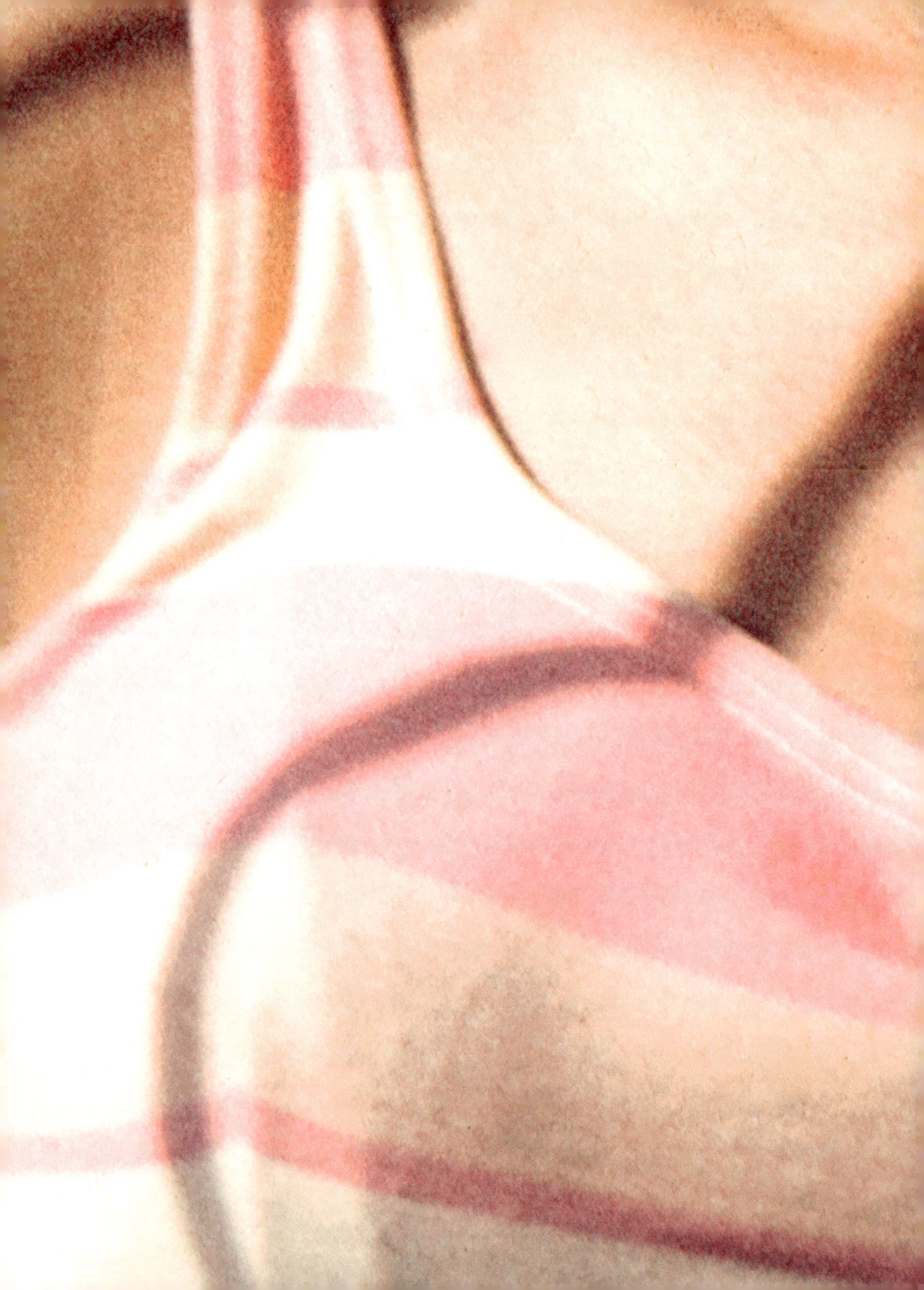

PIA

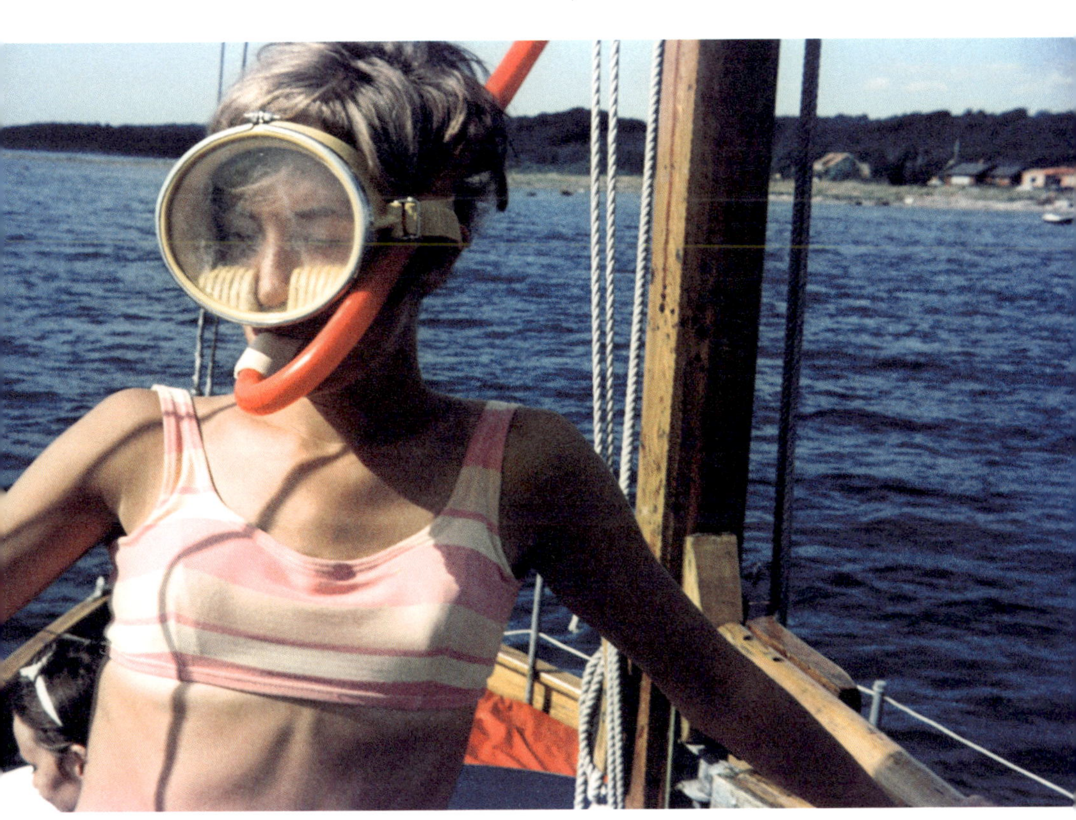

Sjöjungfrun 68-69

The box is labelled in brown ink in the same girlish sloping hand.

The Mermaid must be the name of a boat.

His Swedish grandmother had a summer house on the island of Gåsö.

There is a photo of him painting it; Pia is sitting on the mast wearing white overalls.

There is another of them huddled on deck together, wrapped up against the wind.

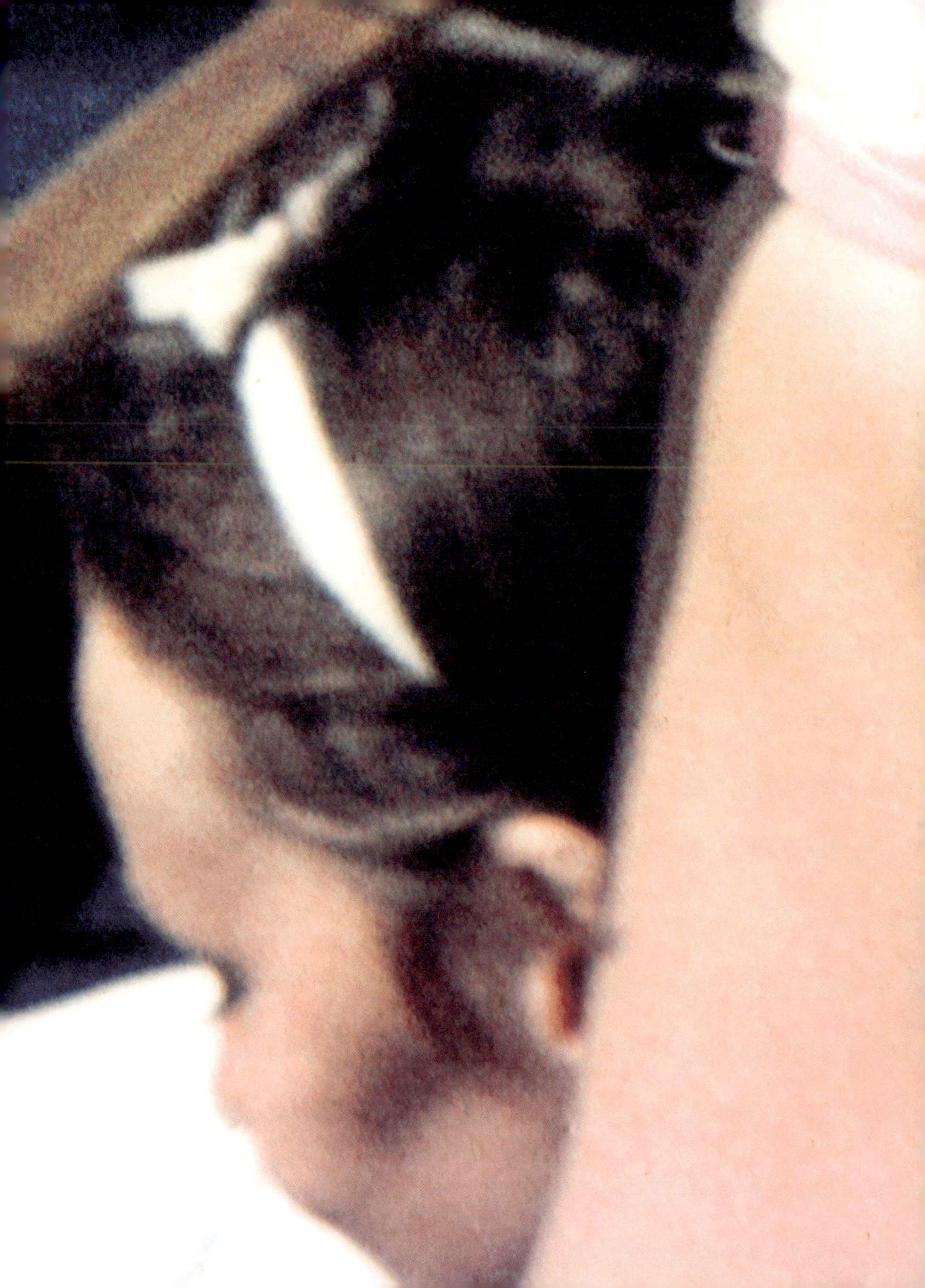

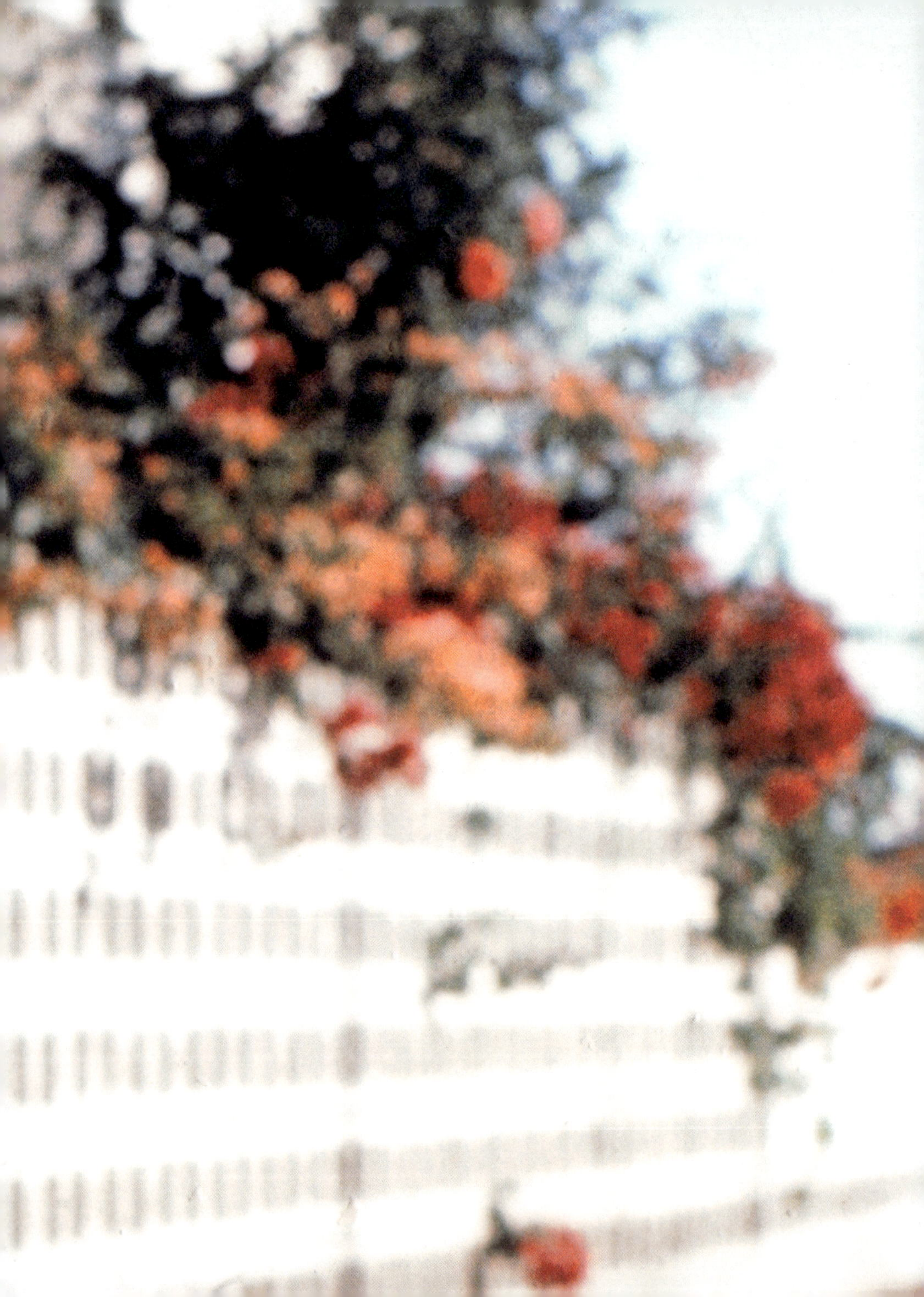

I remember going to a family party,
I must have been ten or eleven.

I learnt (I don't know how) that one of the other
guests had been an ex-girlfriend of my dad's.

She was there with her two children, a boy and a girl.
I recall looking at them sideways through a doorway,
the rooms full of sunlight.

An unfamiliar feeling in my stomach.

PIA

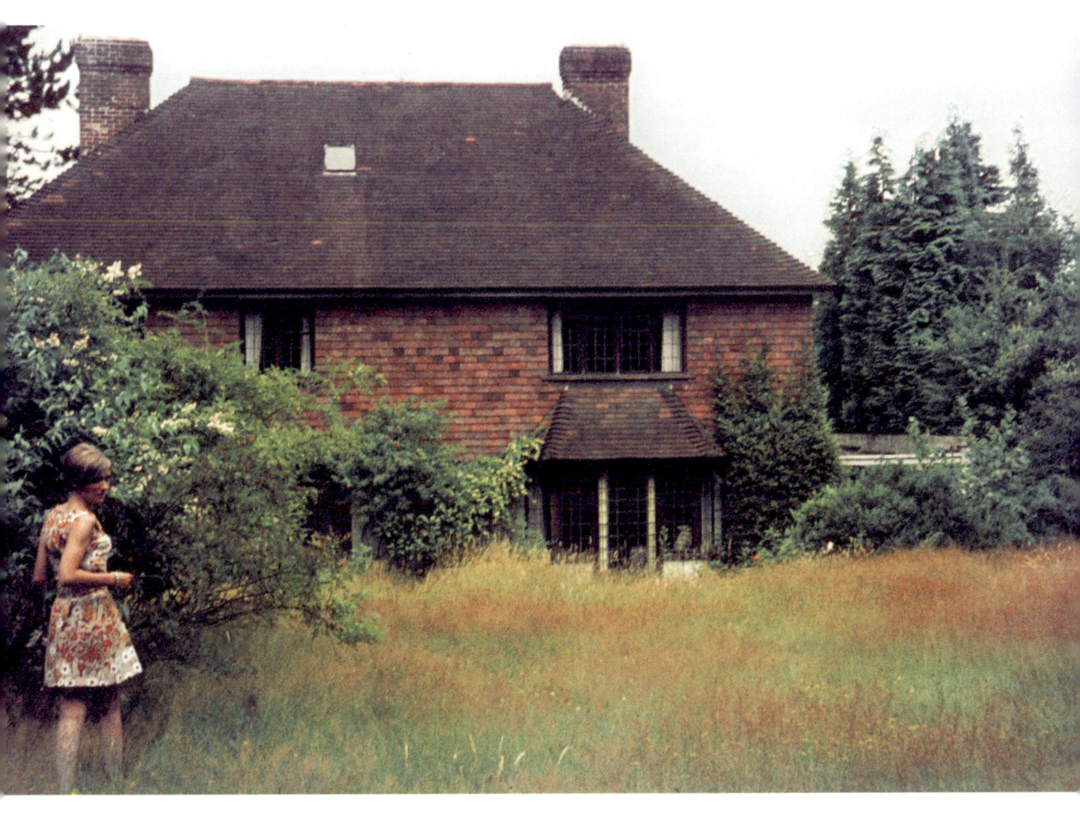

She belongs in a painting,
except for the expression on her face,
which is unmistakeably a scowl.
Her private moment has been intruded upon.

I recognise the house.
It is my father's childhood home.
(He has taken her to England.)
The unruly state of the garden must mean it
is after my grandfather's death in spring 1969.

Unlike my father's usual meticulous composition,
this one feels snatched out of time, the before
and after still vibrating at the edges.

In October of the same year my father will ask
my mother out on a first date.

But for now, it is still summer,
and here is Pia looking irritated.

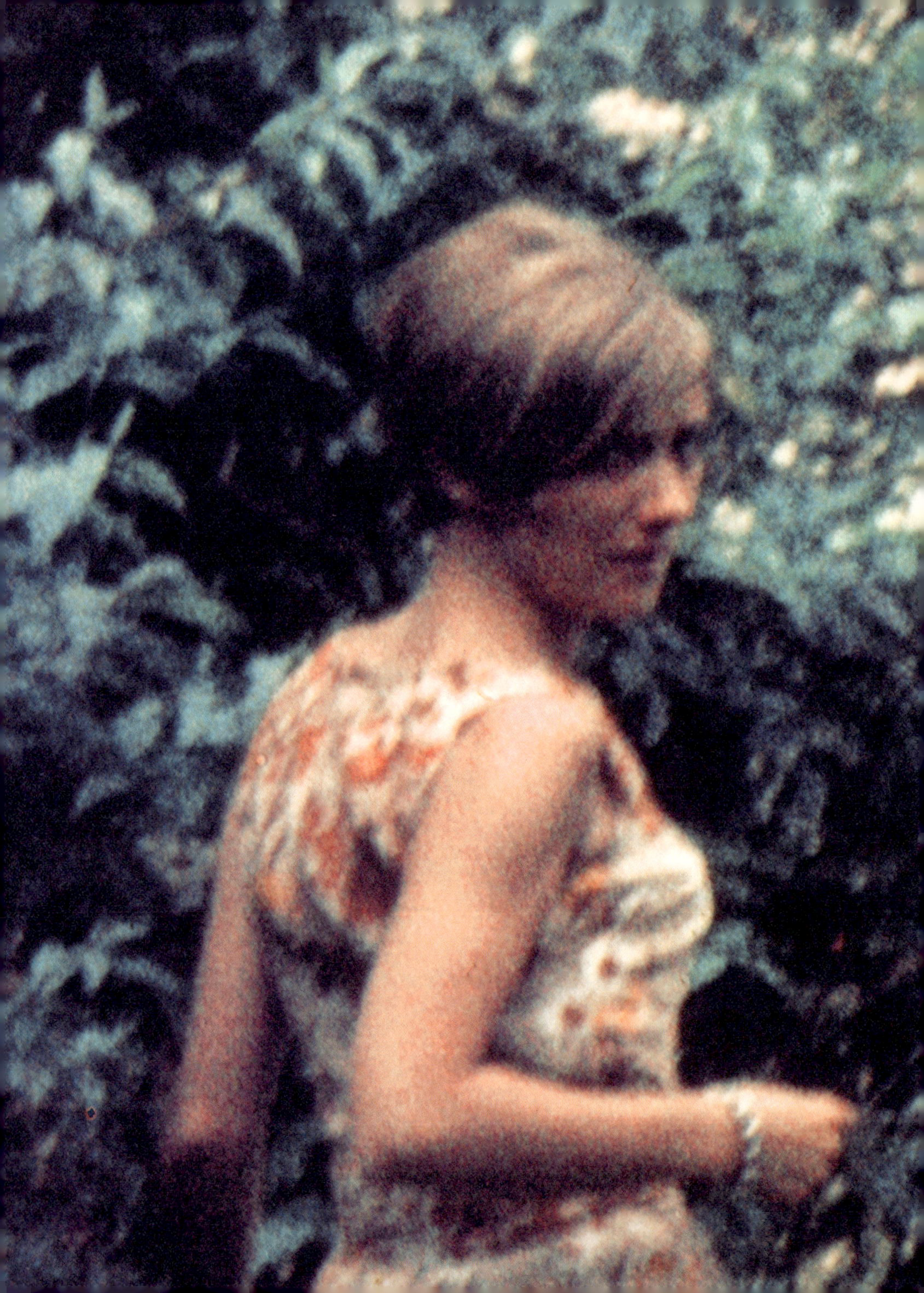

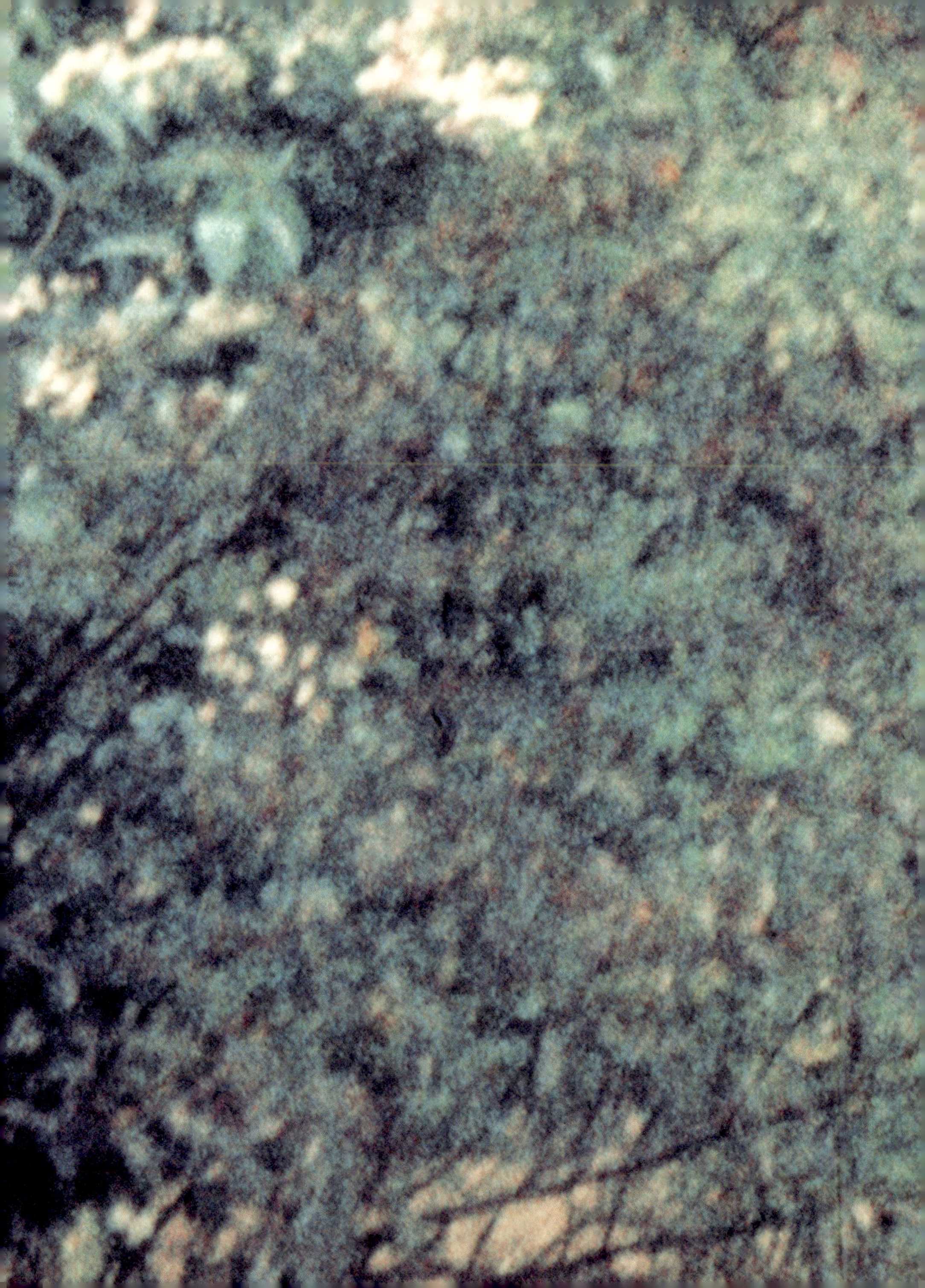

I was driven home after a date
(some kissing in the car).

My father appeared theatrically,
craning through the windows,
making a show of switching on all the lights.

Years later, my husband and I
would pull into the same driveway.
Tired from the journey and parenthood,
desperate not to wake the baby.

Again my father would appear,
switching on the lights, making a noise.
Our efforts thwarted.

There's a photograph of him and Pia standing
in the doorway of what looks like a fisherman's hut.
A small wooden sign reads *Lill-Stugan*.

He's wearing a tweed cap and thick round glasses;
she's wearing a navy headscarf and wire-rimmed spectacles.
They're pretending to be an old married couple.

I don't recall my parents dressing up
as anything other than themselves.
It wasn't their thing.

Except for Christmas Eve.
Father Christmas would visit in person
to hand out the presents.
(I always recognised his shoes though.)

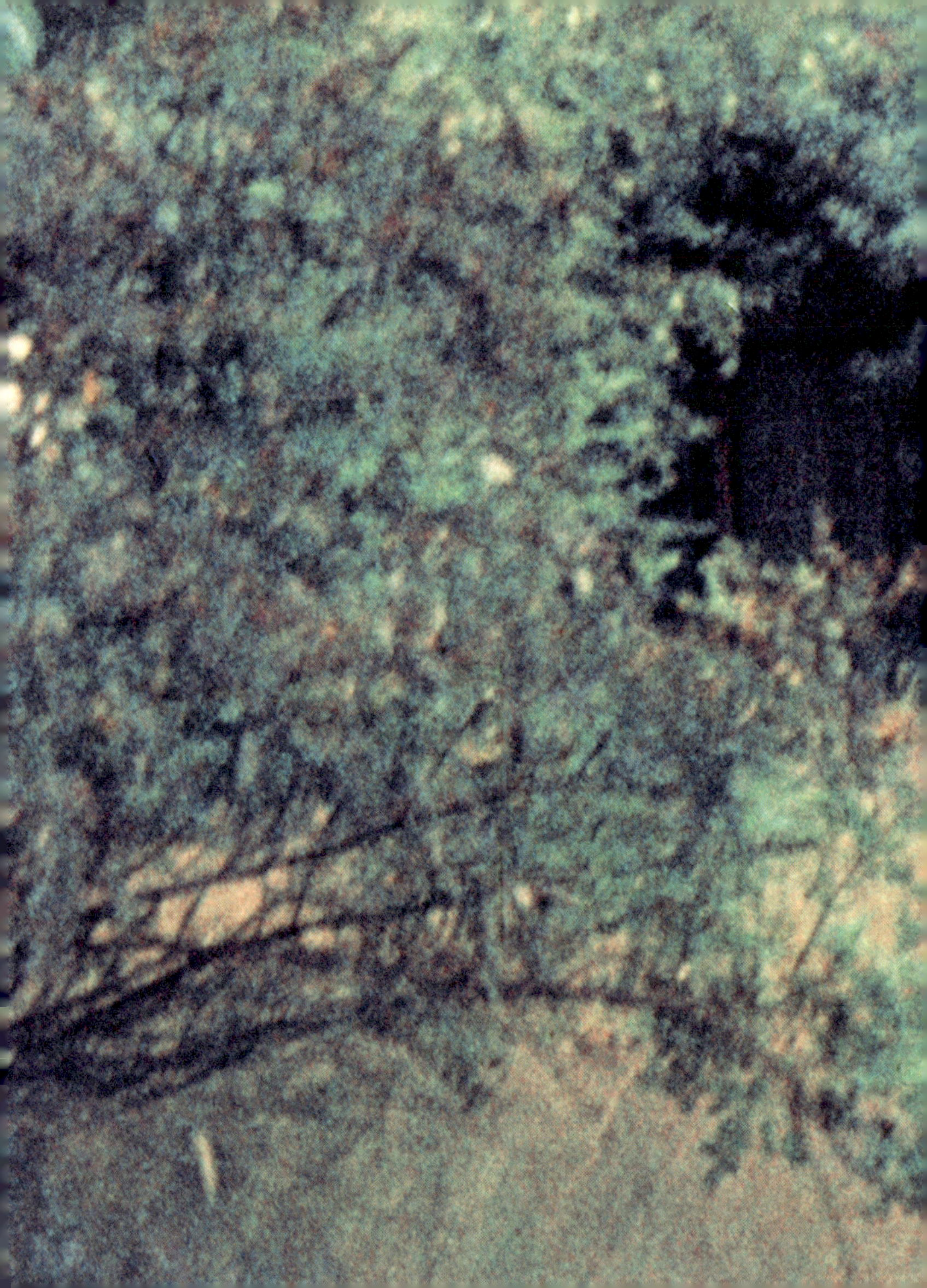

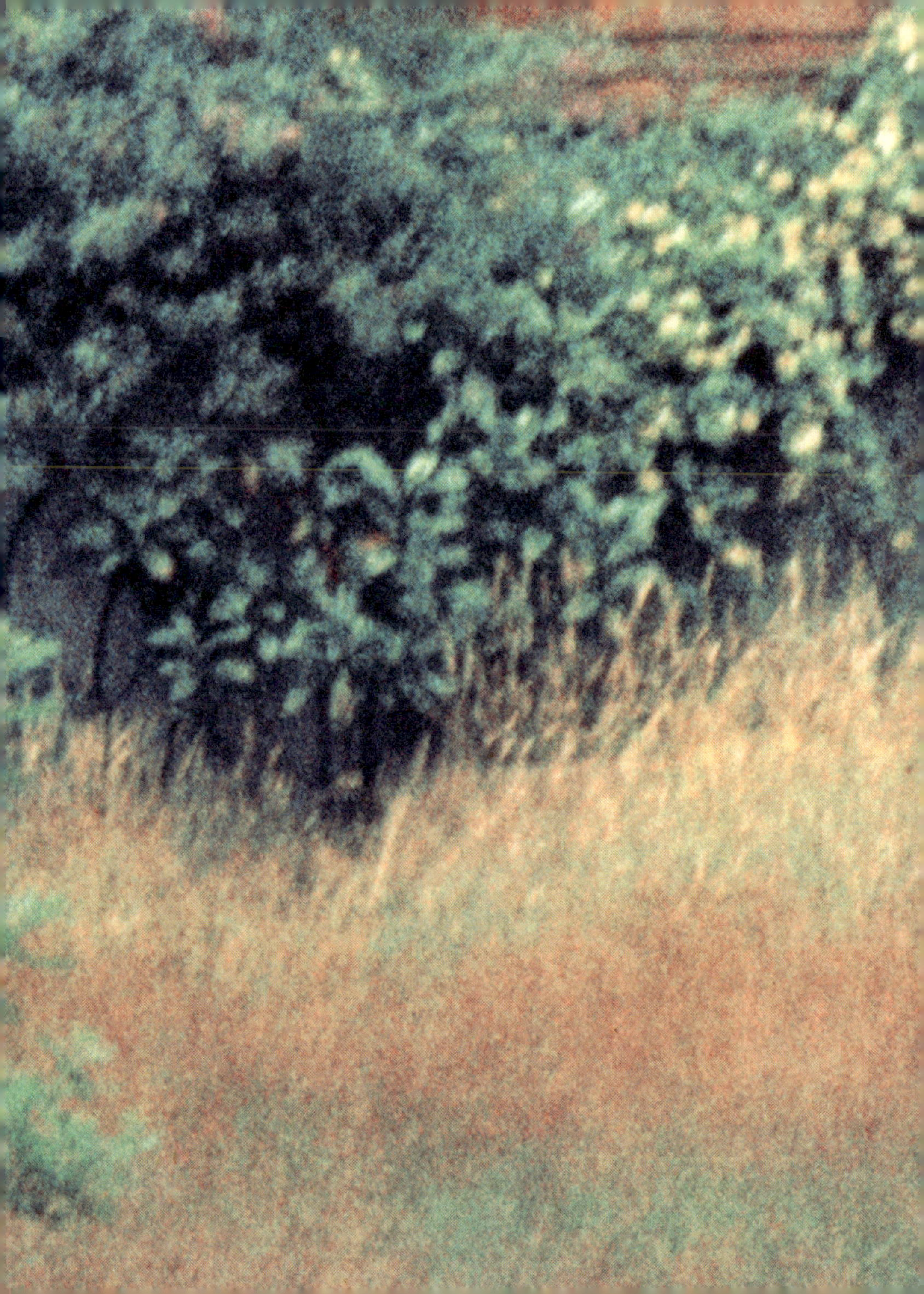

As a child I discovered a small cardboard box
in the upper section of my father's wardrobe.
(It was what remained after his stepmother's
endeavours to eliminate the past.)

It was awkward to reach, and I had to use a chair.
It was crammed with dog-eared letters and postcards.
A good luck telegram from his parents, a black and
white reproduction of marble nudes in an embrace.

A Certificate of Service from Eaton Hall –
Complexion: Fresh, Eyes: Blue, Hair: Fair.
A postcard to his mother, from the Riviera dei Fiori,
the address crossed out and redirected,
Private Patient, Kings College Hospital.

Letters to his father, from Nigeria
(stamps carefully removed).
Congratulations on your engagement.
I think it is wonderful news.

A receipt for his Zeiss Ikon bought in Ibaden.
I have just received the colour slides of some of my
butterflies, and they are absolutely excellent.

Most interesting to me were the handful of
letters from girls with names like Judy and Sue.
There were reminiscences about holidays in Spain
with sombreros, and dinners at The Mermaid in Rye.

There were several from Muffie, hurriedly penned
within a few days of each other one March
(her real name in brackets, should my father's
memory need jogging).

My darling, be good, she crooned.

I teased him about this girl with the silly name.
He didn't mind, but gave nothing away.

He rarely spoke about his past,
The Witch was the exception.

After his father died (of a broken heart),
he never saw his stepmother again.

He drove us past her house once
(it wasn't far away),
just to prove she always kept her curtains drawn,
even during the day.

My mother used to say
it was like having two children.

I gave him margarine fillings,
he taught me to stick chewing gum behind my ear
(which she had to remove with scissors).

But as I grew up
our play became more tricky.

He didn't believe in illness or accidents,
and disliked emotional scenes
(unless they were his own).

I brought my new boyfriend home
(the one I would marry).
We all went to fly a paper kite.

When it was my boyfriend's turn,
the kite blew into a tree.
It became stuck, irretrievably.

My father was incandescent.
His kite (and daughter) ruined.

A week or so before he died
(suddenly, unexpectedly)
we spoke on the phone.

It was different from our usual exchanges
(the small antagonisms that
left me shouting in my sleep).

We talked for a long time
(I cannot remember what about)
but it felt good.

After he died,
I thought about that conversation
many times.

Did he somehow know?

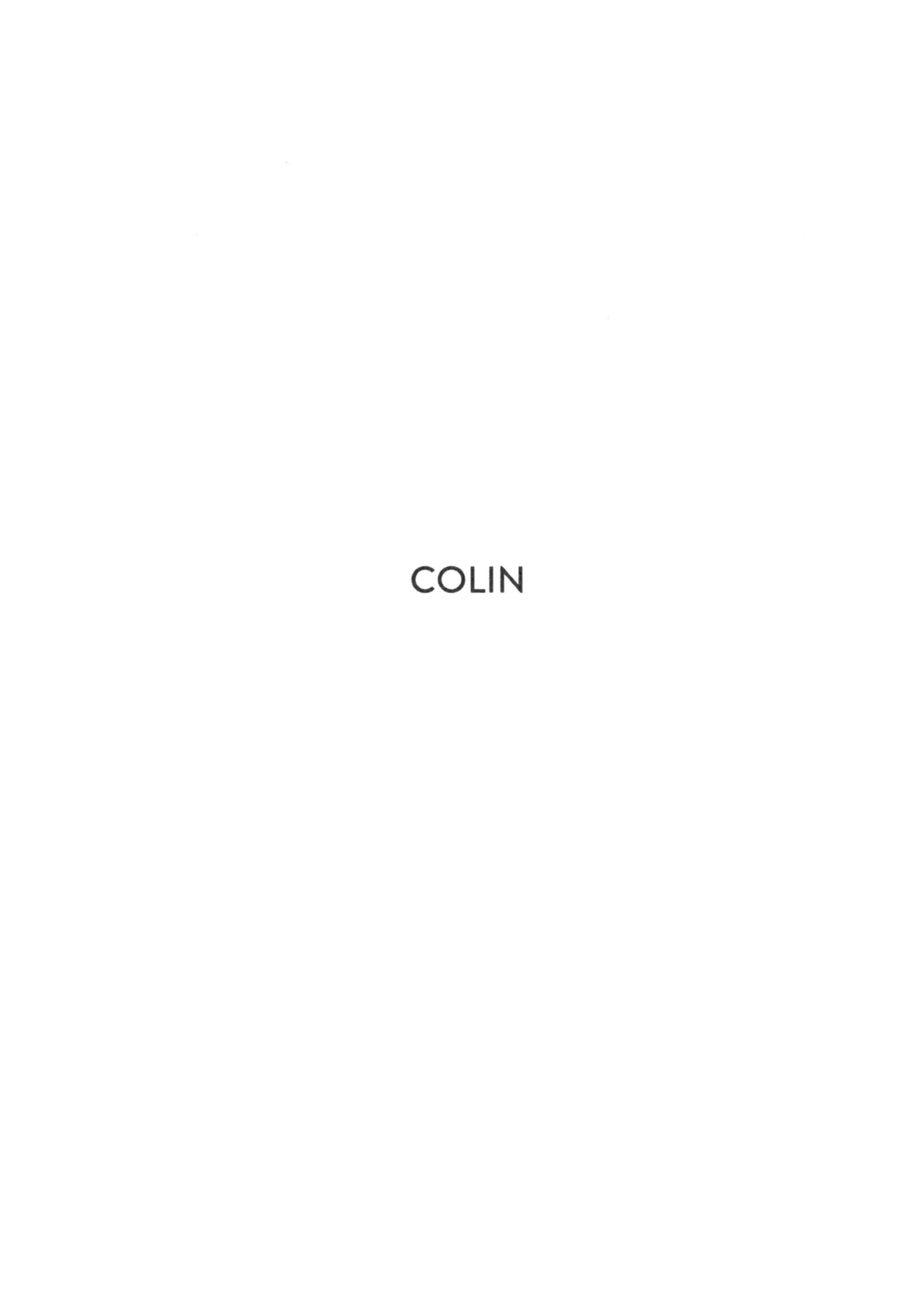

COLIN

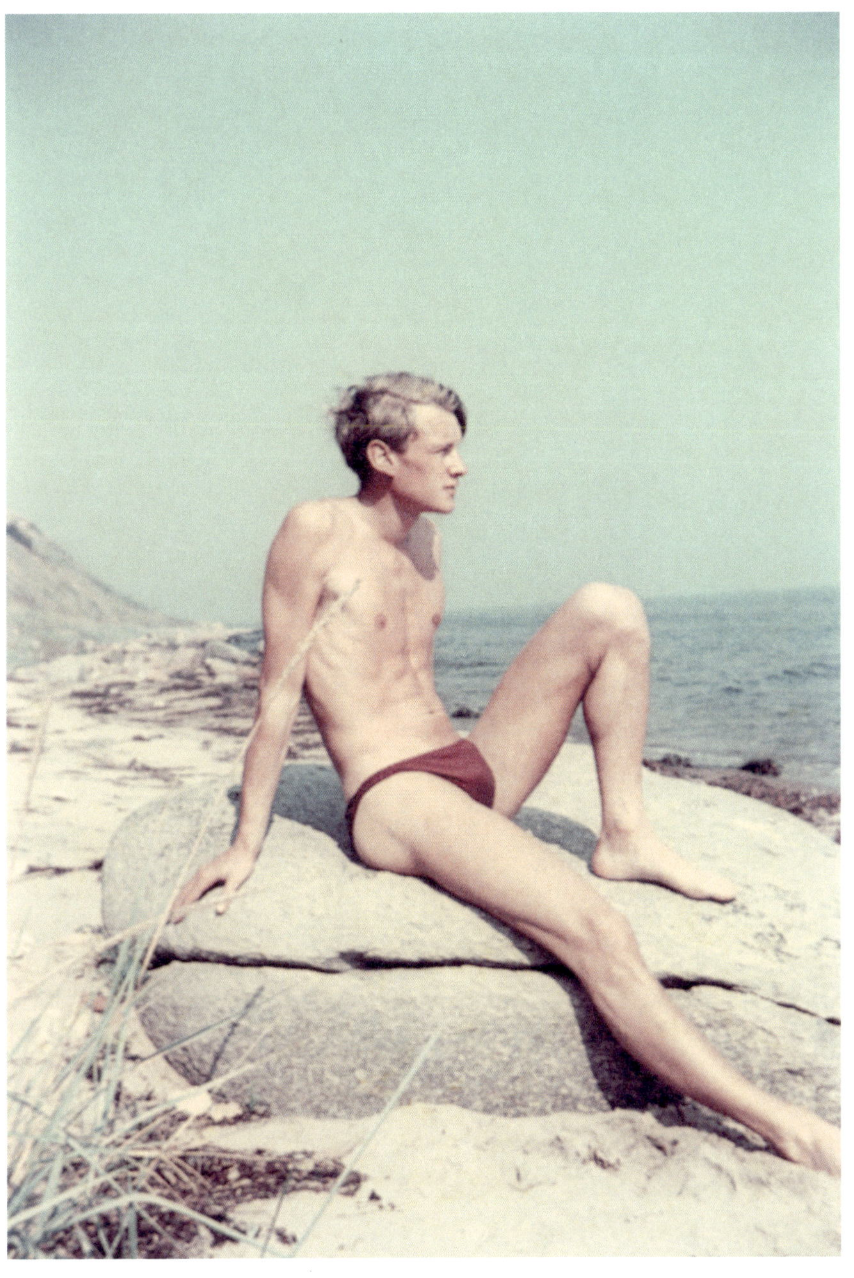

He is sitting on a large rock,
looking determinedly out to sea.
One leg is bent up, while the other
stretches out in the sand.

He is wearing small burgundy trunks,
enjoying the pose.
It reminds me of a scene from
a coming-of-age drama.

He looks like a boy,
though he must already be in his mid-twenties.

He is still becoming.

I am still getting to know him.

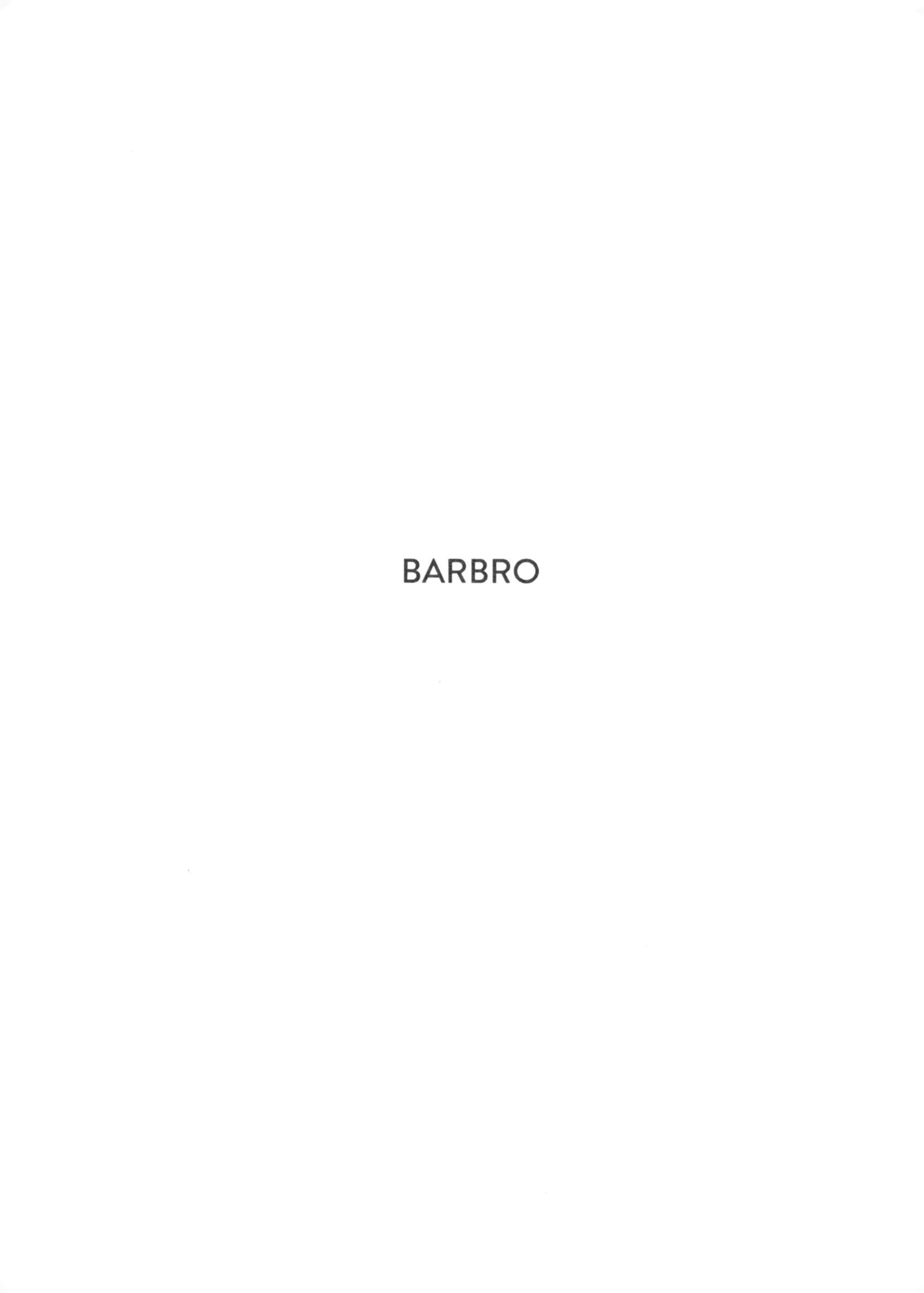

BARBRO

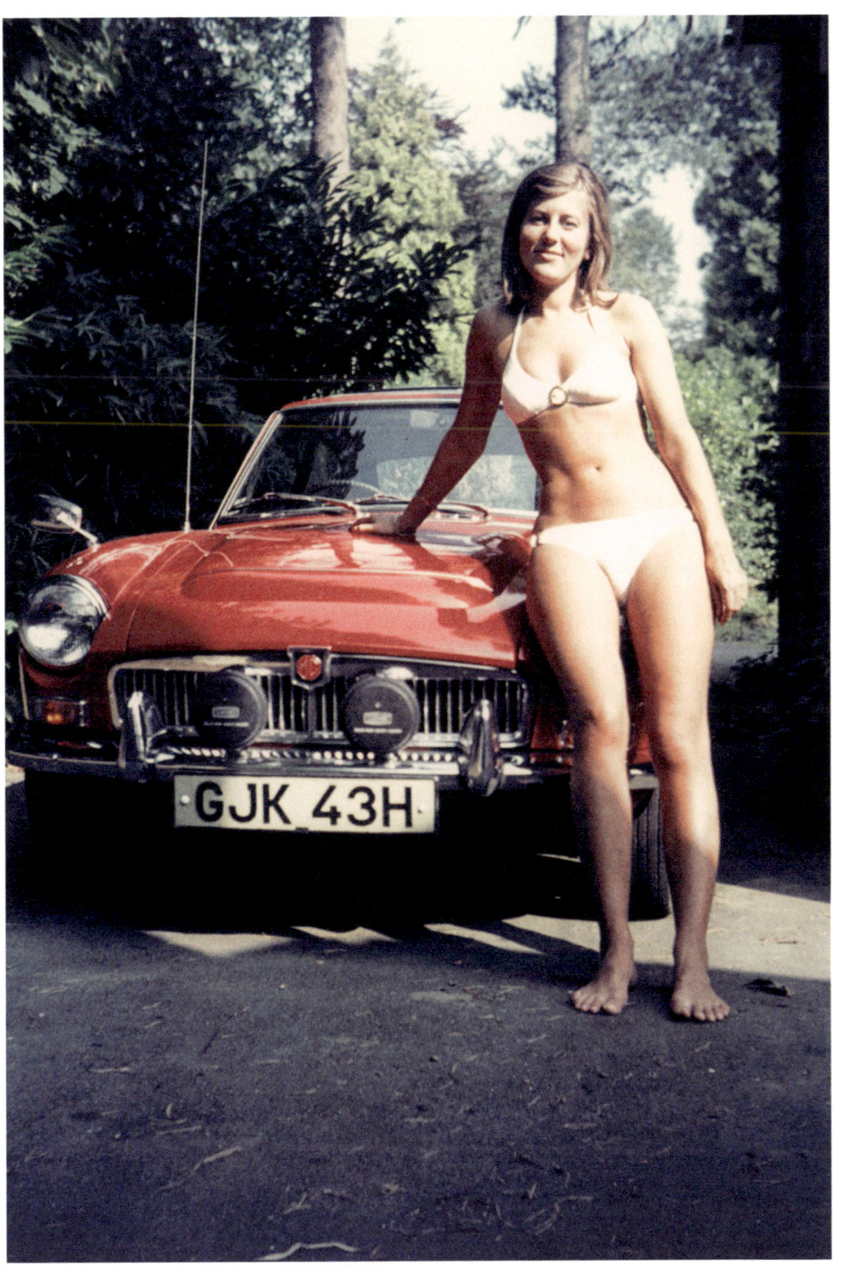
GJK 43H

When I first saw this slide I assumed
it was taken after they were married.

I remember the car.
Squeezing into the back seat with my friend Maddy,
off to see Bambi, clutching our hankies.

But when I asked her, she told me
it was taken before they were married.

She remembered the occasion precisely.

It was the weekend she had come to visit my father,
who had recently returned to live in England.

It was outside his brother's house.

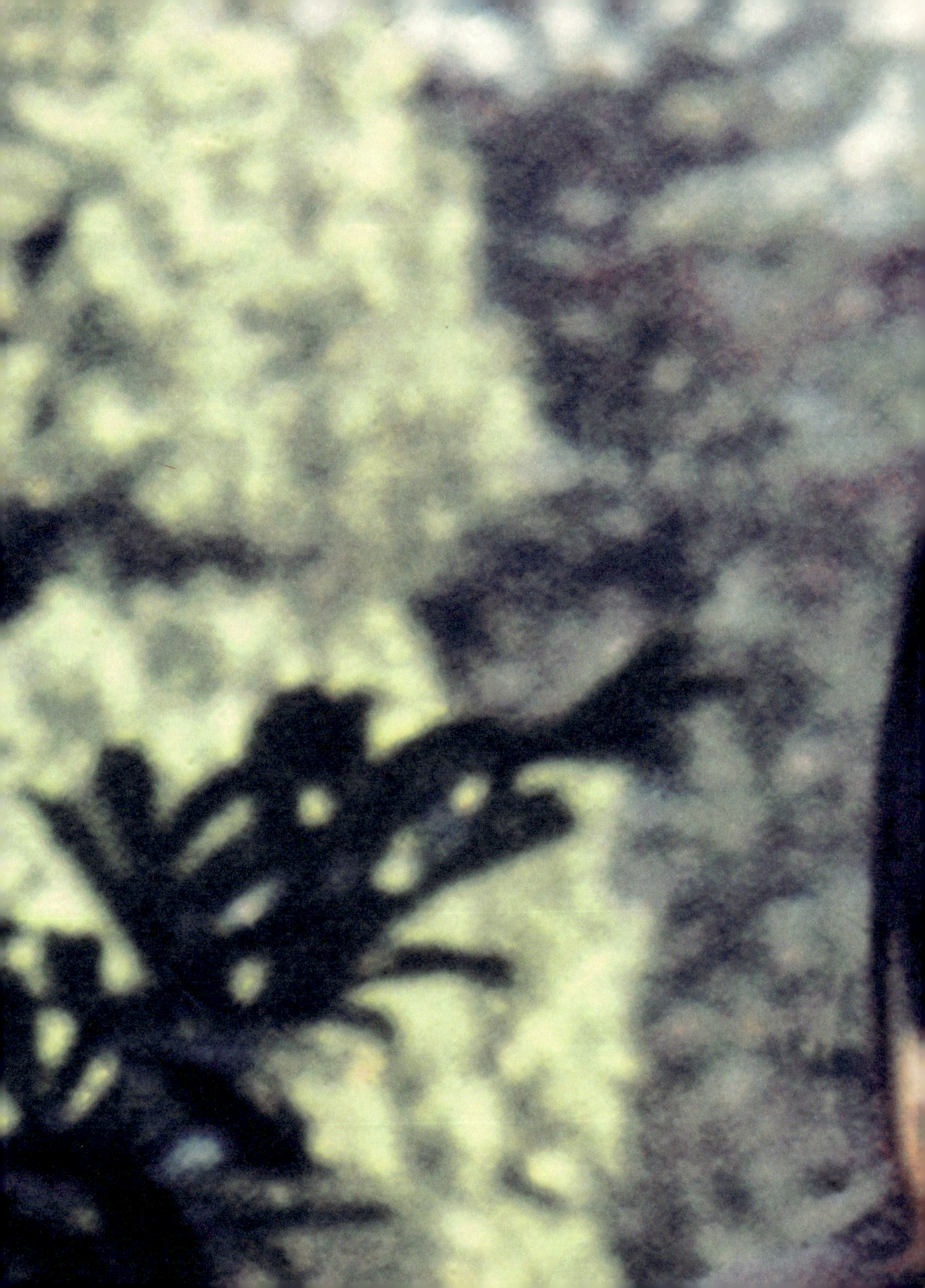

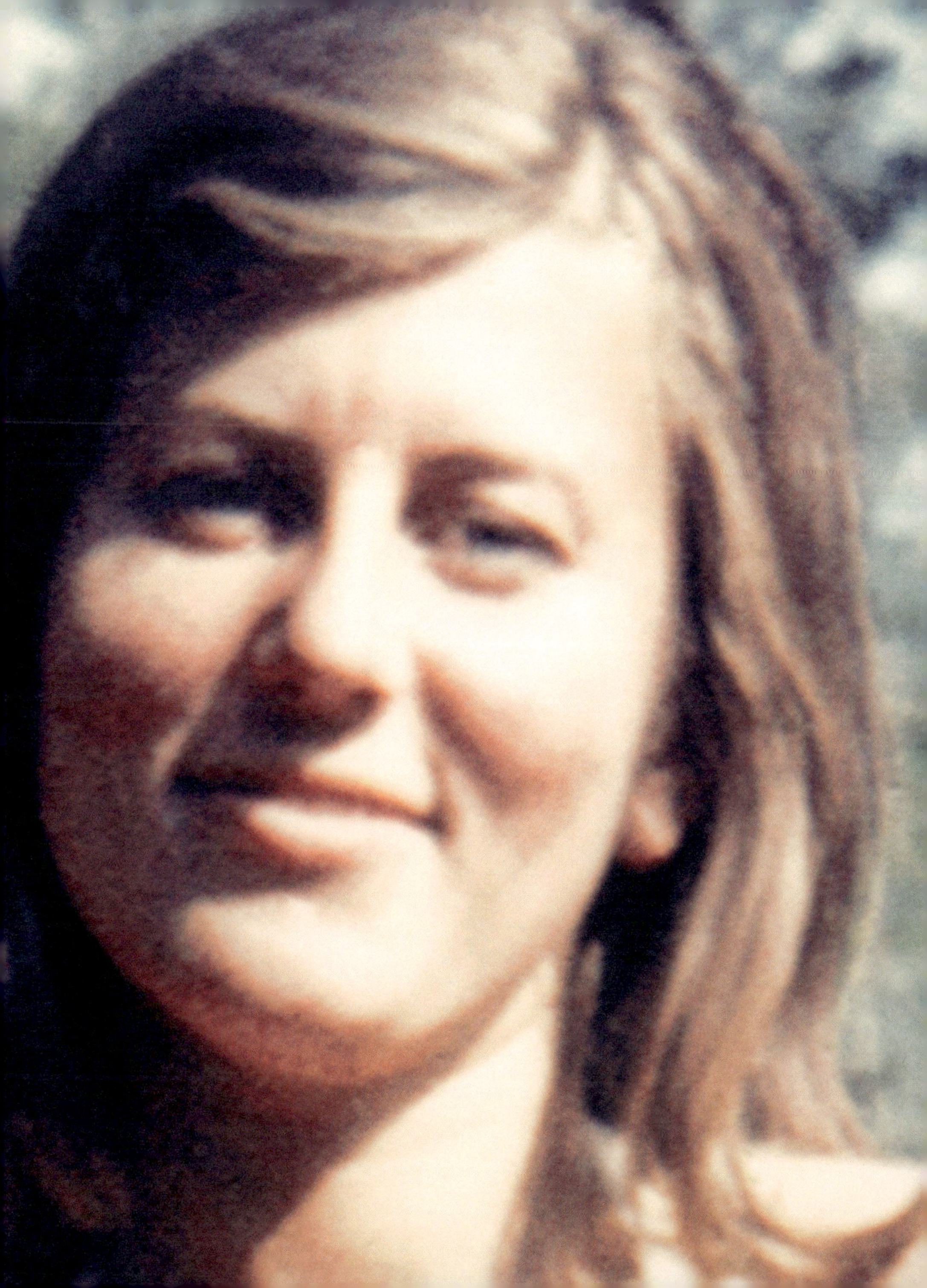

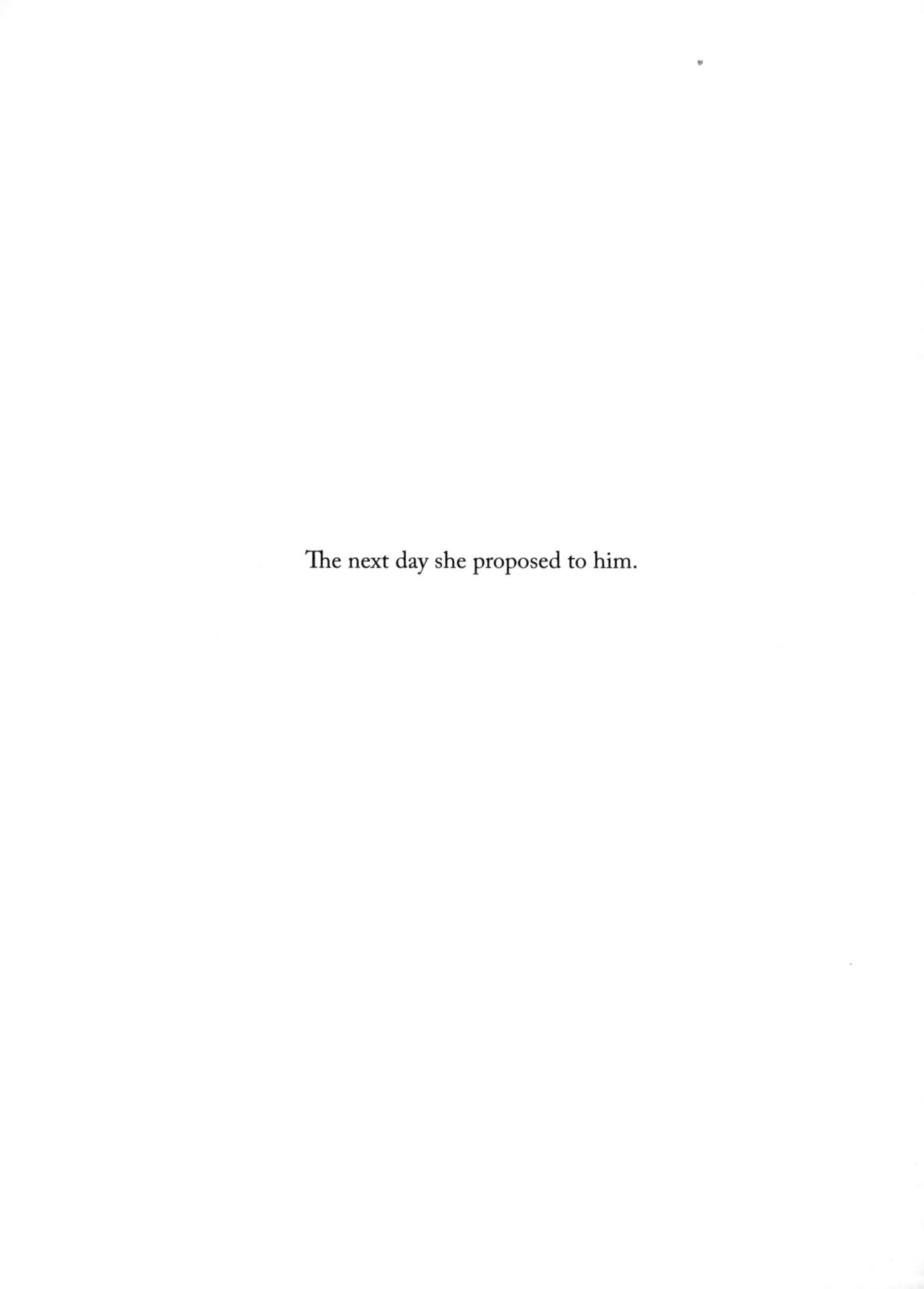

The next day she proposed to him.

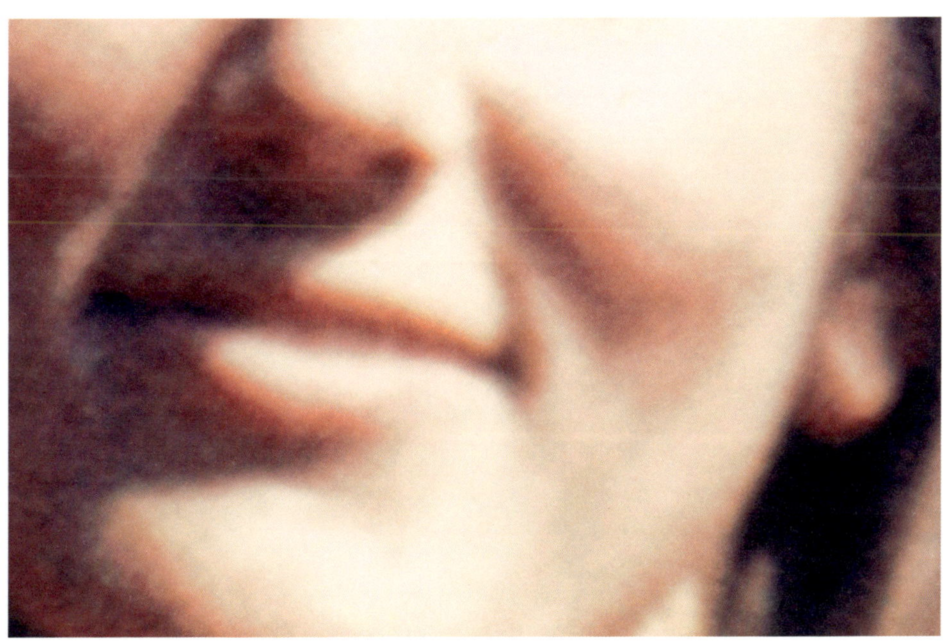

I asked her how these
photographs made her feel.

*You should have seen the
boyfriends I had,* she replied.

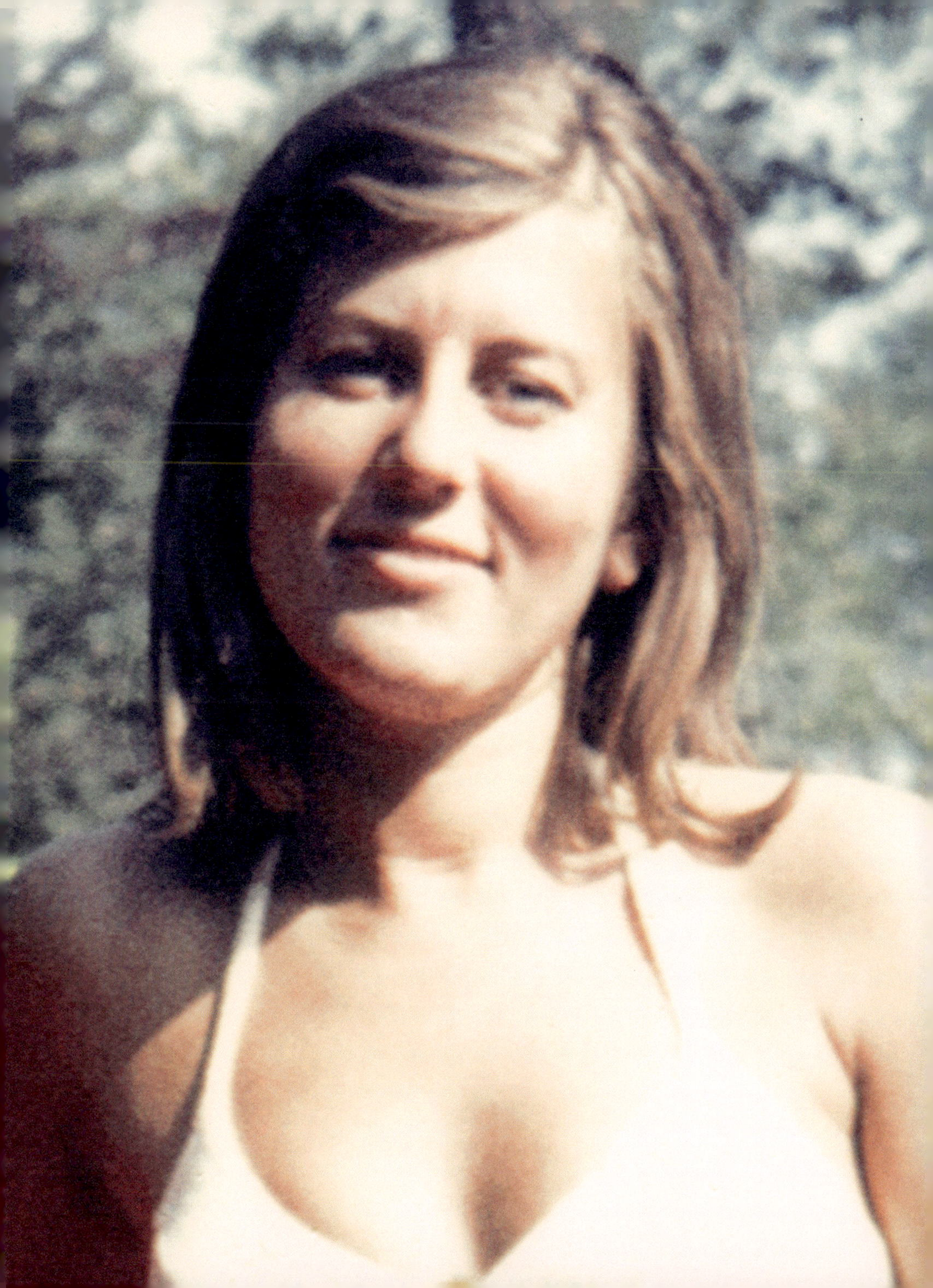

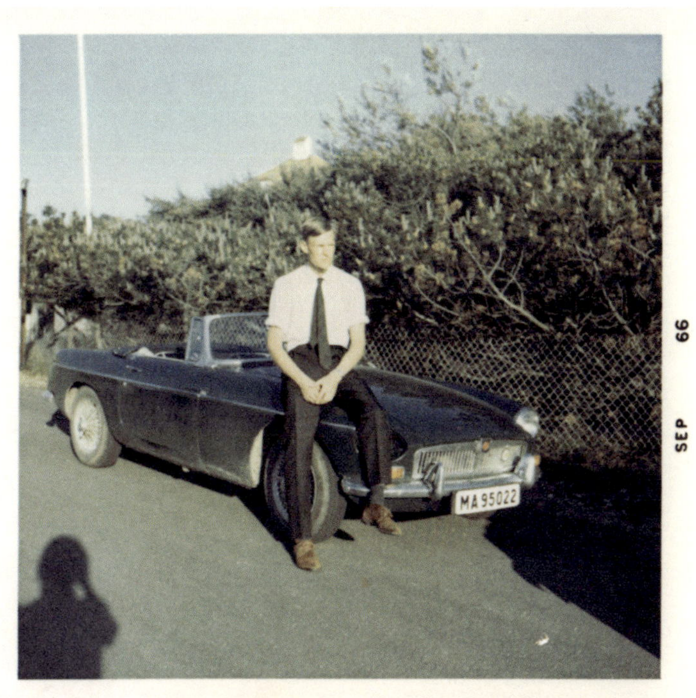
MA 95022
SEP 66

ACKNOWLEDGEMENTS

Sarah Allen for her encouragement
early on and propelling me forward.

Anne Williams, Val Williams, Sophy Rickett,
Polly Braden and Charlotte Cotton
for their sharp eyes and ideas.

Liz Jobey for being a generous mentor and
brilliant editor, and for asking difficult questions.

Dewi Lewis for bringing it to life.

Graham for always believing in me.

First published in the UK in 2024 by
Dewi Lewis Publishing
8 Broomfield Road, Heaton Moor
Stockport SK4 4ND, England
www.dewilewis.com

ISBN: 978-1-916915-04-6

Design: Dewi Lewis & Caroline Furneaux
Print: EBS Verona

www.carolinefurneaux.com